MAPLE

ON

TAP

MAPLE ON TAP

MAKING YOUR OWN MAPLE SYRUP

. . . .

RICH FINZER

ACRES U.S.A.
AUSTIN, TEXAS

MAPLE ON TAP: MAKING YOUR OWN MAPLE SYRUP

Cover photography by:
  Front cover © Thinkstock
  Back cover © Rich Finzer
Interior photography credits appear on page 112

Acres U.S.A.
P.O. Box 301209
Austin, Texas 78703 U.S.A.
(512) 892-4400 · fax (512) 892-4448
info@acresusa.com · www.acresusa.com

Printed in China

Publisher's Cataloging-in-Publication

Finzer, Rich, 1949-

Maple on tap: making your own maple syrup / Finzer, Rich. Austin, TX, ACRES U.S.A., 2012
xx, 116 pp., 22 cm.
Includes Index

ISBN 978-1-60173-034-3(trade)
1. Maple sugar — production. 2. Maple syrup — making.
I. Finzer, Rich 1949- II. Title.

SB239.F56 2012   664.132

TO MY OLD PAL,

PAUL BARTKOWIAK

1936–2011

My dear friend
my sugaring partner
the second father I built from spare parts
my buddy "Doctor Pyro," the true keeper of the fire
R.I.P.

ABOUT THE AUTHOR

During four decades as a writer, Rich Finzer has worked as a newspaper reporter and editor, technical writer and freelancer. His work has appeared in nationally distributed magazines such as *BackHome, Dollar Stretcher, Living Aboard, Life in the Finger Lakes, Upstate Gardeners' Journal, Naval History* and others. He has penned more than 1,000 articles, humorous essays and feature stories. He is also a guest lecturer at Syracuse University on the subject of writing in the commercial environment. He resides on an 80-acre farm near Hannibal, New York, where he's made maple syrup every spring for more than twenty years, since 1991. He loves dogs, cutting his own firewood, and his wife of 36 years (not necessarily in that order). He cannot, however, abide the taste of peas.

ACKNOWLEDGEMENTS

No man is an island unto himself, and no book is the product of a single individual. So I'd like to thank a few folks for helping to make this book possible.

To my wife Delene, for her encouragement while I wrote it, the photos she took on my behalf and for the dozens of orders of fried chicken she reefed (delivered) home to Paulie and me while we were busy boiling.

To the owners of the Countryside Hardware in DeRuyter, New York, for the sugaring advice they freely dispensed to Paulie and me during our early years while we learned the craft of making maple syrup.

To my old pal Paulie, whose enthusiasm, practical suggestions and loyal friendship made the work involved with sugaring a genuine pleasure. Whether stoking the fire, adding fresh sap to the boil, or skimming off the foam, he'd sagely advise; "It's enough of a sufficient amount." That might sound a bit redundant to you, but I'll always treasure those words.

TABLE OF CONTENTS

INTRODUCTION

. . . .

N 1985, I accepted a temporary assignment from my employer and relocated from Upstate New York to New Hampshire. And for the next three years, I became a proud, newly transplanted resident of the Granite State. I have many fond memories of my time there. I met some incredibly interesting people, grew professionally and developed a budding obsession with maple syrup. Alas, in a state full of great maple syrup producing areas, the neighborhood we lived in had been carved from a pure stand of white pine trees. There was not a single sugar maple tree that I could tap in the entire subdivision where I lived. As much as I came to relish the unique taste of pure maple syrup, my stay in New Hampshire just made me want to learn to make my own all that more. It would take another six years of patient waiting for a maple syrup producing opportunity to present itself.

When the New Hampshire work assignment ended and I returned back to my home region near Syracuse, New York, I was more determined than ever to begin making my own syrup. Shortly thereafter, my wife and I purchased an 80-acre farmstead near Lake Ontario and my syruping days began drawing closer. I had great makings in place — for in our yard grew a dozen gigantic sugar maples, each about 100-years-old. In my woodlot were hundreds more. And only three white pines on the entire place! I was finally in sugar maple country. But being a novice, where would I begin?

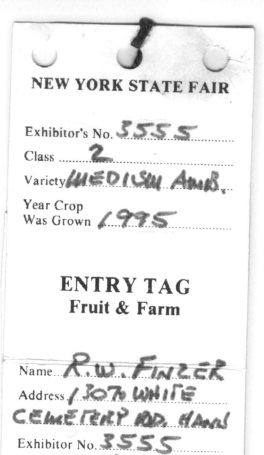

NEW YORK STATE FAIR

Exhibitor's No. **3555**

Class **2**

Variety **MEDIUM AMB.**

Year Crop
Was Grown **1995**

ENTRY TAG
Fruit & Farm

Name **R.W. FINZER**

Address **1307½ WHITE**

CEMETERY RD. HANS

Exhibitor No. **3555**

County **CAYUGA**

FIRST
PREMIUM
—*—
FARM
PRODUCTS
—*—
NEW YORK

Rich Finzer's
First Premium
Award ribbon
and check from
the New York
State Fair.

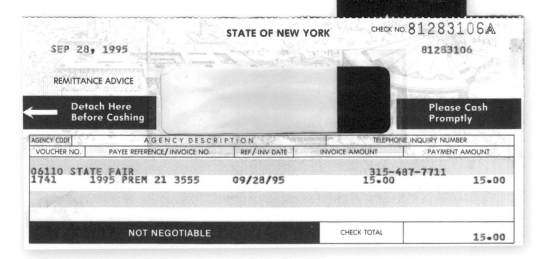

STATE OF NEW YORK CHECK NO. **81283106A**

SEP 28, 1995 81283106

REMITTANCE ADVICE

← Detach Here
Before Cashing

Please Cash
Promptly

AGENCY CODE	AGENCY DESCRIPTION		TELEPHONE INQUIRY NUMBER	
VOUCHER NO.	PAYEE REFERENCE / INVOICE NO.	REF / INV DATE	INVOICE AMOUNT	PAYMENT AMOUNT
06110	STATE FAIR		315-487-7711	
1741	1995 PREM 21 3555	09/28/95	15.00	15.00

NOT NEGOTIABLE		CHECK TOTAL	
			15.00

I started reading everything I could lay my hands on about the process of tapping trees and boiling sap. Some of what I learned was useful, but much of it was not. In retrospect, I had no idea of the challenges ahead that I would face, or the volume of work that was involved. It is said that ignorance is bliss. If that's really true, then I was fast becoming the happiest man on the planet. Fortunately, early on I became friends with my old pal Paulie, who was equally as excited as I was by the prospect of making maple syrup.

Those beginning days were 22 years ago, and since that time, my syruping pal and I long ago achieved our goals of making our own golden delicious maple syrup.

It was an arduous climb up a steep learning curve, but we both had faith that we'd succeed in the end. And we did. In 1995, just five years after we initiated our little enterprise, the medium amber maple syrup we made that spring won the coveted First Premium (blue ribbon) at the New York State Fair. Split 50:50, our $15 cash prize was not even enough to pay for the supplies that year, but that blue satin ribbon was worth a king's ransom, and boosted the daylights out of our self-esteem. Our ragtag little 24-tap operation had competed head-to-head with commercial producers and beaten them! Following that victory, the additional awards we subsequently earned and the experience we garnered over the next 15 years of production eventually became the catalyst for this book.

If your goal is learning to make your own maple syrup, then I promise you that this little book will explain exactly how to do that. Everything in here represents the way I've learned to make maple syrup. There won't be any confusing terminology, no obscure references, no tasks you can't accomplish or obscure acronyms to figure out — just easily understood, cold, hard facts coupled with field-tested techniques that work. And just for the record, all production figures, statistics, prices, etc. are based upon my own 24-tap backyard operation.

Will your syrup win a blue ribbon? Heck, I don't even know if that's your plan. But I can tell you this, if you follow the directions in this book, you'll stand a much better chance of accomplishing a blue ribbon than if you don't. Am I bragging? Nope. Like Dizzy Dean once remarked, "If you done it, it ain't braggin.'"

Let me congratulate each of you for deciding to make your own maple syrup. While the work is hard, you will attain a great sense of personal triumph when you serve your own homemade/handmade syrup to friends and family. It's another step toward increased self-sufficiency, sustainability and personal growth. You are about to become part of a uniquely North American tradition. And I wish each of you the greatest degree of success in your endeavors.

RICH FINZER

GLOSSARY

SINCE MAPLE SYRUP PRODUCTION IS such a unique pursuit, there are a host of specialized terms associated with it. Some are slang expressions, while others represent proper scientific or maple syrup industry terminology. This listing should provide you with enough to keep the terms all straight and prevent any confusion.

ACER: The botanical genus of all maple trees.

ACER NIGRUM: Botanical name of the black maple.

ACER SACCHARUM: Botanical name of the sugar maple.

ACER RUBRUM: Botanical name of the red maple.

AUGER: Deeply fluted, extremely sharp drill bit used to tap maple trees.

ARCH: The lower unit on a maple sap boiling rig that contains the firebox.

BUD SAP: The late-season maple sap containing budding hormones.

EVAPORATOR: Any container used to boil off maple sap.

GOLDEN DELICIOUS: Slang term for maple syrup.

MUD SEASON: Slang term describing the end of winter or beginning of spring when the frost comes out of the ground and maple syrup is made.

NITRE: Condensed mineral salts that precipitate out of boiling sap. These impurities must be filtered out prior to bottling or canning.

GLOSSARY

RESERVOIR: A tank or container used to preheat sap before adding it to the boil, also referred to as a pre-heater.

REVERSE OSMOSIS MACHINE: Specialized apparatus with a semi-permeable membrane used to separate water from raw maple sap, commonly known as an "RO" machine.

RIG: Slang term for the arch and evaporator.

SPILE: Old-style galvanized or stainless steel maple tap.

SUGAR BUSH: Collective term describing any large stand of sugar maples.

SUGARMAKER: The official term coined by the Vermont Maple Sugar Makers' Association for its members.

SUGAR SAND: Slang term for nitre.

SUGAR RUN: Slang term for a period of time, generally 24 to 72 hours, when temperatures remain continuously above freezing and tap holes drip like crazy. Under perfect conditions with no wind and falling barometric pressure, a 24-tap setup might gather as much 60 gallons of sap during a good "run" of sugar. If you've tapped early enough in the season, a lucky sugar maker may be treated to two or three of these blessed events.

SUGARING OFF: Slang term for making maple syrup.

TAPPING: The act of boring holes and inserting taps into a maple tree.

CHAPTER 1

MAPLE SYRUP
IN NORTH AMERICA

WHEN THE EARLY European settlers arrived on North American shores, they discovered that the native peoples living in the northeast knew how to make a sweet, delectable tasting syrup from the native sugar maple trees. Lacking iron pots, in the Spring the tribes made this syrup by filling up hollowed log troughs with tree sap and dropping fire-heated rocks into the liquid to boil away the water. It must have been an incredibly time-consuming process with no quality control. The new settlers soon recognized maple syrup as a food source and a tasty sweetening agent that they could use to supplement their subsistence diet in this foreign land. The settlers quickly realized the economic potential of making maple syrup. Maple syrup represented a brand new sweetening source that was relatively easy to transport and offered the possibility of being a good cash crop both in the New World and for those selling it back home in the Mother Country.

This spurred them to improve the maple syrup making process significantly. For the settlers, just having proper cooking pots would have made a tremendous advantage over the hot rocks and log troughs method and enable the settlers to have better and better results.

Upon realizing the economic potential of maple syrup, the colonists laboriously

Maple syrup is a unique product produced exclusively in North America.

dug, balled, and transported over 30,000 sugar maple saplings to England. The British planted them in formal plantations and eagerly waited for the day when the trees would reach tapping size. Unfortunately the English winters were so mild that the trees never achieved full dormancy. No dormancy meant no sap run and consequently no maple syrup production. In the end, the trees were cut down and used to heat the pot stills used for producing Scotch whisky.

It was realized then (and still is true today) that maple syrup is a unique product produced exclusively in North America.

OTHER MAPLE TREES

All maple trees belong to the botanical genus Acer, and the sap of all maple trees contains some percentage of maple sugar. The sap of the sugar maple (*Acer saccharum*), contains the highest concentration, typically about three percent. This means

40 GALLONS OF RAW MAPLE SAP = 1 GALLON MAPLE SYRUP

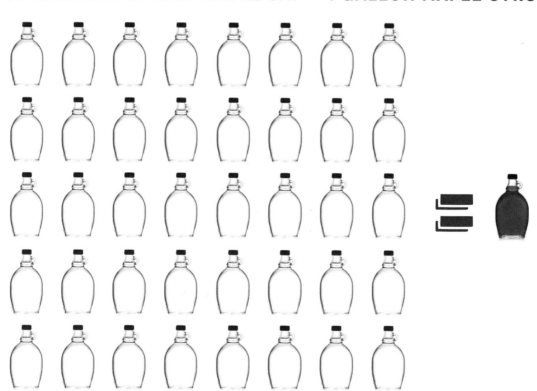

that on the average you'll need 37 to 40 gallons of raw sap to produce one gallon of syrup. Over the course of a single season, an individual tree tap will produce roughly enough sap to yield one quart of syrup. So based upon my 24-tap operation and assuming I boil three to four times, I'll produce a maximum of about six gallons each spring. To illustrate the sap to syrup ratio again, bit on a smaller scale — if you have

You've got to boil a river of maple sap to produce a puddle of maple syrup.

a 20-ounce soda bottle filled with sugar maple sap, then when it has been boiled down to syrup, the yield would be slightly more than 1 tablespoon. I like to think of it as … you've got to boil a river of tree sap to produce a puddle of maple syrup. The wonderful maple flavor and the syrup is already there in the maple sap coming straight from the tree, your task as an amateur producer is to get rid of everything (water and salts mainly) that isn't this syrup.

Many factors affect the sugar content in the collected sap. The sugar content depends upon where your trees are growing, the weather conditions — especially the amount of winter snow cover, how warm the daytime spring temperatures rise and the small genetic differences between individual maple trees. Trees growing in a dense woodlot will begin their sap run a bit later than a single lone tree in a field due to the fact that the shade keeps them dormant longer. In an open area such as your side yard, with ample sun exposure, the sap run will commence much earlier. But keep in mind, this stuff is not an exact science, and the sugar content and sap yield will actually vary from one tree to another from year to year. A high sugar content and a good sap yield seems to be part luck, part Mother Nature and part mystery — take your pick.

The growing ranges of all three maple species overlap one another and one woodlot may contain all of them.

DON'T OVERLOOK RED MAPLES

If the area where you reside does not have a large population of sugar maple trees, don't despair. The sap from red maples (*Acer rubrum*) can still be boiled down to make syrup instead. But you will need much more of it. The sugar content of the raw red maple sap is roughly half that of sugar maple, meaning you'll need twice as much to produce a gallon of syrup. Red maple has a wide growing range, with early running sap. Even if there are no sugar maple trees to tap in your neighborhood, expanding your options to include red maples, means you can still sugar off. Additionally, red maples grow much faster than sugar maples (but don't live nearly as long) — potentially giving you trees to tap sooner. If you have both red and sugar maple species present, blend the sap together. The syrup you make will handle just the same. More than likely, your taste buds won't know the difference either.

CONSIDER BLACK MAPLE

While perhaps not as well known as sugar maple or red maple, the black maple tree (*Acer nigrum*) can also be tapped for making syrup. Nicknamed "black sugar maple" or "hard maple," the Vermont Department of Forests, Parks and Recreation website *www.mapleinfo.org*, says that the sugar content of black maple sap is roughly equivalent to that of sugar maple. Fortunately, the growing ranges of all three of these maple species (sugar, red and black) overlap one another and one woodlot may contain all of them. (See the Additional Resources section at the back of the book for more information about each maple species.)

To find out more about the growth characteristics, leaf shapes or general physical configuration of maple trees, I'd recommend purchasing a good reference book. The best one I know of is the *National Audubon Society Field Guide*

① VERMONT
890,000 GALLONS

NEW YORK ②
312,000 GALLONS

③ MAINE
310,000
GALLONS

WISCONSIN ④
117,000 GALLONS

⑤ NEW HAMPSHIRE
87,000 GALLONS

MICHIGAN ⑥
82,000 GALLONS

⑦ OHIO
65,000 GALLONS

PENNSYLVANIA ⑧
54,000 GALLONS

to *North American Trees: Eastern Region.* Published by Alfred A. Knopf, Inc., this 700+ page guide is loaded with color photos of maple leaves (including autumn and spring foliage), maple seeds, bark, form and species descriptions. Those with no interest in making syrup, find that this is still a terrific book to own.

SOME GEE-WHIZ NUMBERS

Since the amount of tree sap flowing is dependent on many factors including Mother Nature, nationwide, syrup production quantities also vary from year to year. Since 2000, the U.S. average annual production is well over two million gallons. According to the USDA, in 2010 the top eight producing states (ranked in order) were Vermont, New York, Maine, Wisconsin, New Hampshire, Michigan, Ohio and Pennsylvania.

Interestingly, if you add up the totals from these top-producing states, they barely reach the national average of two million gallons. The reason is that an extremely early arrival of warm springtime weather made for a disastrous 2010 sugaring season in many of the top-producing states. For some producers, both amateur and commercial, syrup production fell by as much as forty percent (mine certainly did)! And

A HIGH SUGAR CONTENT AND A GOOD SAP YIELD SEEMS TO BE PART LUCK, PART MOTHER NATURE AND PART MYSTERY — TAKE YOUR PICK.

note that the production totals listed are commercial statistics reported to the USDA by the Agriculture Departments of the top eight producing states. The numbers do not include the syrup produced by the thousands of amateur backyard and small wood-lot producers — just like you and me.

So just how ubiquitous is the sugar maple tree? How interwoven into our culture is this tree species? Well, it's the official state tree of New York, Vermont, West Virginia and Wisconsin. The sugar maple leaf is also the national symbol of Canada.

Old style galvanized sap buckets — the traditional method of sap collection. The massive maple pictured here is nearly five feet wide at the base and can easily accommodate four taps.

The five lobes of
a sugar maple leaf.

And it deserves to be, as the province of Quebec produces roughly 6.5 millions gallons of syrup annually — over three times the total U.S. production. Additionally, the U.S. Forest Service estimates that in New York alone, the population of sugar maple trees exceeds 150 million. And when was the last time you drove through a village, town, city or hamlet just about anywhere in the U.S. that didn't have a Maple Street?

Maple syrup is also imbued with numerous unique characteristics. A teaspoon of syrup contains fewer calories than an equal amount of ordinary table sugar. Plus research funded by the Federation of Quebec Maple Syrup Producers revealed that maple syrup contains newly discovered chemical compounds with anti-oxidant or anti-inflammatory properties like those found in blueberries and other so called "super foods." And even if that wasn't the case, maple syrup is still the best friend a plate of pancakes ever had!

People in North American have been making pure maple syrup for at least 400 years. It's a product that is uniquely ours because of our climate and the presence of sugar maple trees. Collectively, after four centuries, we've gotten pretty good at making the delectable stuff. So there's no reason to think you can't do it too.

CHAPTER 2

START BEFORE YOU BEGIN

FOR A FIRST-TIME sugar maker, the time to prepare for sugaring off is a year or two before you actually intend to commence tapping and boiling. You've got lots of planning to do and more than likely, numerous items to acquire. Most importantly, you've got to read this book and everything you can lay your hands on about making syrup. As you read, there are many questions to answer that you should be thinking about. These questions will help with the planning process.

1991 (Year One): Yes, we really boiled down in a wash tub in the back yard.

Do you intend to become a serious sugar maker, or simply wish to try it once just for the fun of it?

How many taps do you intend to hang?

What kind of tapping system will you employ; spiles and buckets, sap bags or something else?

Do you know how or where to acquire the equipment and supplies you'll require to properly tap maple trees and sugar off?

Prior to boiling, where and in what type of container(s) will you store your collected sap?

Do you intend to pursue this venture alone or will you seek out a willing co-conspirator?

How much syrup do you want to make? »

The point to all these questions is not to dissuade you, rather simply to explain that you've got heaps of variables to consider. Think about it this way, you could just as easily go into a grocery store, buy some maple syrup, take it home, put it in a glass pitcher, and tell the world you made it yourself. Who would know? So the message I'm attempting to convey is this; the eventual outcome you wish to achieve is predicated upon planning, education and a brutal level of personal honesty. So right upfront, if you don't want to deal with the significant amount of heavy lifting that making maple syrup entails, then buy it at the grocery. Because let me tell you, make no mistake about it, as a backyard producer, making syrup is just plain old hard work!

Will you boil outside or do you own an outbuilding you could use as a makeshift sugar house?

What will you use for an evaporator?

Can you acquire enough fuel to fire your evaporator rig, and at what cost or inconvenience?

Are you going to do the "finishing," and if so, where will you do it?

Do you intend to bottle or can your syrup?

Do you have enough sap collection containers?

How much money are you prepared to spend to buy the things you'll likely need?

How much raw physical labor and time are you willing to commit to your syrup making enterprise?

Will you be tapping sugar maples, black maples, or red maples?

Over the course of the season, do you know how much syrup each individual tap will yield when the sap from it is boiled to syrup?

Basic Sugaring Supplies & Gear

- ☐ **TAPS**
  either plastic, steel spiles or aluminum spouts

- ☐ **COLLECTION CONTAINERS**
  buckets, sap bags, plastic jugs or pails

- ☐ **SAP AUGER AND DRILL**

- ☐ **SAP STORAGE CONTAINER(S)**

- ☐ **EVAPORATOR**

- ☐ **WOOD**

- ☐ **A BOILING SITE**
  (any place except the kitchen, see Chapter 10 for the reasons why)

- ☐ **SYRUP CONTAINERS**
  canning jars, plastic jugs, glass bottles or steel cans

- ☐ **LIDS OR SCREW-ON CAPS**

- ☐ **FILTERS**

- ☐ **STOCK POT(S)**

- ☐ **CANDY THERMOMETER**

Oh, and you're going to need some equipment too. So here's a starter list.

Again, this list is not meant to intimidate, rather it's here to educate you and justify the one to two years of preparation time needed that getting ready may require. Chapter 15 has a more extensive list of equipment and supplies along with an idea of costs. If you scour the want ads or check online you may be able to purchase some of these items at a slight discount, or acquire used equipment. After a fashion, preparing to sugar off is somewhat akin to building a city. And we all know how a city goes up; brick by brick.

CHAPTER 3

FUEL FOR SAP BOILING

FOR THE TYPICAL backyard sap boiler, wood is the most practical fuel source. If your sugar bush is also a woodlot, you are lucky and can harvest your own. For unlike money, wood does grow on trees! Many commercial producers also fire their rigs with wood as well, though natural gas, propane, heating oil and waste oil are also often used instead. If you only have a few maple trees, as an alternative you may be able to swap some syrup with a neighbor in exchange for wood and the privilege of tapping their trees. Keep in mind, a commercial sugaring operation incorporates its fuel costs into the price of its syrup, but you may not have this option. Your goal is to be as self sufficient as possible while minimizing expenses. With a goal of getting the most out of your fuel, I have included a table with various firewood types and their respective BTU energy content ratings. Keep in mind that not every tree species grows everywhere, but all grow somewhere in sugar country; another reason the *National Audubon Society Field Guide to North American Trees: Eastern Region* book is such a handy item.

With my sap boiler I demand a hot fire and plenty of flames. Consequently I fuel my small evaporator unit with a mixture of both hardwood (mainly black locust) and softwoods. I usually cut and split my wood a year before I intend to use it and age it indoors until it is tinder dry. If your evaporator arch is relatively small, the pieces of wood

Several small pieces of wood have a greater combined surface area than a single larger piece. So split your wood into finer pieces and build a big, roaring blaze.

you place inside should be small as well. Several small pieces have a greater combined surface area than a single larger piece. So split it into finer pieces and build a big, roaring blaze.

If you are boiling down 45 gallons of sap, you'll need about 200 pieces of finely split wood. Split it ahead of time, as you'll have plenty of other chores to do on the day you boil. If you are employing an arch like the one pictured here, and assuming a boil of 40 to 50 gallons, you'll need approximately ¼ face cord each time. So based upon your seasonal syrup goals, plan accordingly and plan well ahead.

A nice stack of finely split black locust, red oak, white spruce and pin cherry that will make for a hot fire. I usually burn 150 to 200 pieces this size while boiling down a 45-gallon batch of maple sap.

With a proper fire and plenty of fuel, hot is what you got!

FIREWOOD BTU RATINGS PER CORD

SPECIES	MBTU*	POUNDS PER CORD (DRY)
OSAGE ORANGE	32.9	4,728
SHAGBARK HICKORY	27.7	4,327
EASTERN HOP HORNBEAM	27.1	4,016
BLACK BIRCH	26.8	3,890
BLACK LOCUST	26.8	3,890
HONEY LOCUST	26.5	4,100
APPLE	25.8	3,712
MULBERRY	25.7	4,012
AMERICAN BEECH	24.0	3,757
NORTHERN RED OAK	24.0	3,757
SUGAR MAPLE	24.0	3,757
WHITE OAK	24.0	3,757
WHITE ASH	23.6	3,689
YELLOW BIRCH	21.8	3,150
TAMARACK	20.8	3,247
GRAY BIRCH	20.3	3,179
PAPER BIRCH	20.3	3,179
WHITE BIRCH	20.2	3,192
CHERRY	20.0	3,120
GREEN ASH	19.9	2,880
BLACK CHERRY	19.5	2,880
BLACK ASH	18.7	2,924
RED MAPLE (SOFT MAPLE)	18.1	2,900
JACK PINE	17.1	2,669
NORWAY PINE	17.1	2,669
PITCH PINE	17.1	2,669
BLACK SPRUCE	15.9	2,482
EASTERN WHITE PINE	14.3	2,236
BALSAM FIR	14.3	2,236

*MBTU = million BTUs per cord

BTU data courtesy of World Forest Industries from their website, *www.worldforestindustries.com*

If you are boiling down 45 gallons of sap, you'll need about 200 pieces of finely split wood.

CHAPTER 4

ROOKIE YEAR MISTAKES & HOW TO AVOID THEM

N 1991, WHEN I decided to "sugar off" for the first time, I didn't have a clue what the outcome would be. I also didn't have a proper evaporator, any experience or anyone to lean upon for help other than my partner Paulie, and he'd never made maple syrup before either. We were rank novices and we made more mistakes than you could imagine or shake a stick at.

HERE ARE THE ROOKIE MISTAKES WE MADE:

1 TOO DEEP

That first year, we boiled in a galvanized washtub (really). I degreased it and scrubbed the inside shiny, but I made one critical error. I filled it too full with maple sap and it took extra time for the sap to begin bubbling. Now we know the trick is to keep the sap level relatively shallow — roughly three inches in depth at most. I'd filled ours to where it was deep enough to bathe in, wasting a lot of both fuel and time.

2 TOO WINDY

Since we were in a bind with all of our 1-gallon plastic storage jugs being filled with maple sap, we were forced to boil on a cloudy and windy day. As a result, much of the heat our fire generated simply blew away. So if you must boil outside, find a sheltered location where the wind won't steal the heat away. And make sure you never run out of storage containers. Too many is heaps better than not having enough.

NOT ENOUGH WOOD

I had no idea how much wood it would take to boil off forty gallons of sap. I'd accumulated a wood ring filled with pallet scraps and somehow deemed that I had enough, and I was wrong. Between the strong gusty winds and too much sap to boil, we quickly ran out and I was forced to cut up scrap wood I'd put aside for another project. The bottom line, always have more wood than you could possibly burn. For me that equates to a full-face cord of split 4 inch rounds of black locust, oak, beech, softwood or pallet scraps.

IMPATIENCE

I was firmly convinced that once we got color in the maple sap, we were well on our way to making syrup. Wrong again. Oh, we had a nice medium amber color, but we still had another fifteen gallons of sap left to boil down. What I hadn't bothered to acquire yet was a decent thermometer. Our boil temperature was probably at 213 F, but no more than that. In essence, we were merely boiling amber-colored water. The sugar content was just beginning to come up to syrup level and the steam did have a distinct maple smell. But we misread those signs and assumed we were almost done boiling when in fact we still had a ways to go. Once again, we were mistaken.

LACKING PROPER TOOLS FOR FINISHING

For those unfamiliar with the term, "finishing" a batch of sap into syrup consists of closely monitoring the temperature, filtering the finished product, grading and bottling it. For backyard and small-scale producers, this is usually

I HAD NO IDEA HOW MUCH WOOD IT WOULD TAKE TO BOIL OFF FORTY GALLONS OF SAP. THE BOTTOM LINE, ALWAYS HAVE MORE WOOD THAN YOU COULD POSSIBLY BURN.

So what did we do wrong that first year? The answer is practically everything. About the only thing we did correctly was to pick the right time to tap.

A red maple leaf.

performed inside on the kitchen stove. As we lacked a thermometer, Paulie and I did the next best thing we thought, we guessed. We also lacked proper filters and ended up straining the liquid through several layers of muslin. The result — it almost nearly worked. We strained out the heavier deposits of nitre (sugar sand) ending up with beautifully clear amber-colored stuff that looked and smelled almost like maple syrup. Bottling and sealing the jars was the only thing that went smoothly. We were finally done, had taken a few test tastes and were absolutely certain we'd made maple syrup. A week later I took a sample to a commercial operator I'd met previously and asked for his opinion of our finished product. His response dealt me a disappointment of galactic proportions! We'd succeeded in making maple "something" but it sure as heck wasn't syrup. I now think of it as a "close but no cigar moment." I hated breaking the bad news to Paulie, but the sad fact was we'd failed. Some sugar makers we were.

OUR FIRST ATTEMPT — WHAT WE DID WRONG

FUEL

At the risk of sounding redundant, be certain you have plenty of wood. What you don't use on your first boil, you'll need for a second go at it. If you are planning to boil outside, creosote buildup won't be an issue, so be sure to include wood from pitch-rich trees such as seasoned white pine, pin cherry or white spruce. All three tree varieties burn hot and fast, and when boiling sap, flame is the name of the game.

THERMOMETER

Since Paulie and I failed to understand that sap doesn't begin the transition to syrup until the temperature reaches about 218°; we erroneously calculated we were done boiling too early. Now we know that decent syrup doesn't happen until the finishing temperature is slightly above 220° F. Therefore, a rugged and accurate candy thermometer is a must item to have. Since we have not sold any of our syrup, we usually now ran the temperature up to 221° F before filtering. The finished product is super-sweet, which is exactly how we liked it. The thermometer we use costs about $20. A digital model, if you prefer this, is over four times as expensive. For an amateur producer, digital is an unnecessary extravagance.

DECENT FILTERS

Initially we simply didn't realize how difficult it would be to filter out all of the sugar sand. What we needed was a supply of Dacron fiber filtering cones. At current prices, expect to pay around $20 per dozen. After a couple of years struggling with other filter materials, we finally bought some in 1993, the first year our syrup won a ribbon at the New York State Fair and have been happy we did ever since.

A proper candy thermometer like this one is a "must have" to get started.

KNOWLEDGE

My partner and I began making maple syrup mired in pools of ignorance. We'd both read a book on sugaring, which was akin to reading a book about riding a bicycle and figuring that you knew how to do it. Consequently, we both "flew over the handlebars" numerous times. So my best advice is to invest a year or two in the company of an experienced producer, either commercial or amateur. Ask to hang around and help. From my experience, arriving with a cold drink is an excellent form of introduction. And while you're there, lend a hand and be sure to ask your body weight in questions. Sugar guys can always use a spare pair of hands and we sure enjoy sharing our expertise. Did I mention that sugaring is extremely thirsty work?

As we ended our first year, with many lessons learned, we unsealed our jars, re-boiled, re-filtered and re-bottled what little syrup we had left. Calculating the total effort we'd expended, we could just as easily have raised the Titanic. So what did we do wrong that first year? The answer is practically everything. About the only thing we did correctly was to pick the right time to tap.

My partner and I began making maple syrup mired in pools of ignorance.

CHAPTER 5

WHEN TO TAP YOUR TREES

A S WITH OTHER outdoor pursuits, deciding when to tap your trees is a matter of good timing, experience and a keen awareness of the weather conditions in your area. It's not a case of a bell going off somewhere and everybody taps on the same day. The date varies not only from state to state but by geographic areas within a single state. As an example, folks living in Connecticut, with its relatively mild winters, may be drilling holes by late January, while those of us living in snowy, upstate New York usually have to wait a few weeks longer. So how did Paulie and I decide when to tap our trees that first year? Simple, we asked the owner of a local commercial sugaring operation. His advice to us was to tap on the weekend closest to Valentine's Day, and with few exceptions we have stuck to that every year.

Deciding when to tap your trees is a matter of good timing, experience and a keen awareness of the weather conditions in your area.

VALENTINE'S DAY

I say with few exceptions, because if the temperature is in the single digits on Saturday, February 14, there's no point in drilling holes. The trees will not have broken their dormancy yet, and no sap is going to be running. There is also another factor to consider when settling on a tapping date, and that is the location of your trees. If your maples are in a deep woodlot or growing in a hollow, the ground will warm more slowly because it will take extra time for the sun to begin melting off some of the snow cover and reawakening the trees. Conversely, the trees on my farm are on the highest ground and widely spaced so they break dormancy earlier.

The best advice I can give regarding tapping dates is to ask an experienced local expert, and I prefer the counsel of commercial sugar makers for this. It's literally their business to know and I've always accepted any of their collective wisdom as gospel. And why shouldn't I? I'm not a competitive threat, because I don't sell any syrup. Furthermore, with an annual production of maybe six gallons as opposed to perhaps several thousand gallons, I'm considered like a gnat on an elephant's backside, too small to even warrant consideration, much less inspire worry. However, if there are no local commercial operations nearby, don't despair. There are three other equally useful sources for advice.

> THE BEST ADVICE I CAN GIVE REGARDING TAPPING DATES IS TO ASK AN EXPERIENCED LOCAL EXPERT, AND I PREFER THE COUNSEL OF COMMERCIAL SUGAR MAKERS FOR THIS.

OTHER SOURCES OF ADVICE

Contact your local cooperative extension office if you live anywhere in maple syrup country. Someone on the staff is bound to have answers for you. There's another equally valuable source of information as well — the agriculture or horticulture departments of colleges and universities. Strictly as an example, and only because I reside about 70 miles from campus, I contact Cornell University. Over the years, the agriculture students and faculty there have studied and researched every facet of maple syrup production. Additionally, they run a sugaring operation of their own.

Lastly, my advice is to keep your eyes open. If all of a sudden you start seeing sap buckets appearing on maples trees in your area, it's probably time to tap yours too.

CHAPTER 6

TAPPING
& SAP COLLECTION

• •

WHEN TREE TAPPING time finally rolls around in your area, every amateur maple syrup maker has four challenges to combat: wind, inclement weather, insects, and a big time commitment dedicated to sap collecting. As I now begin my twenty-second season of sugaring, I'm struck by how many mistakes I made when I got started doing this as well as how many time- and money-saving techniques I have now learned from these many years of experience. So here are a few important points to keep in mind when you've decided to take the plunge and "sugar off" for yourself.

SAP COLLECTION SYSTEMS

Every sap collection system shares two common elements — tapping the tree and collecting the sap. Everyone must tap his or her maples to release the sap and there must be some kind of container to collect the sap as it drips out. But as a backyard or small-scale producer, you won't be running a tubing network attached to a vacuum pump. Instead, you need to think about your sap collection on a small scale with the

- BUCKETS
- SAP BAGS
- PLASTIC MILK JUGS
- 5-GALLON PLASTIC JUGS
- 4-GALLON PLASTIC JUGS

emphasis on economy, simplicity and practicality. Your goal is to minimize or eliminate having to transfer sap from one container to another and to accumulate enough to boil. So I am going to share four basic methods you might pursue, along with the costs, pitfalls and benefits associated with each. I'll use our 24-tap operation as the measuring stick with which to compare all the different collection systems.

When tree tapping time finally rolls around, every amateur maple syrup maker has four challenges to combat: wind, inclement weather, insects, and a big time commitment dedicated to sap collecting.

BUCKETS

Traditional sap collection is done using either metal spiles and nine quart galvanized metal buckets or plastic taps and 3-gallon translucent plastic buckets. Both of these types require lids. For each tree tap, the metal buckets, lids and spiles will cost about $26 plus tax. For us, this was multiplied twenty-four times at an expense of about $650.

For the plastic equivalent, each rig will cost roughly $14 plus tax (or about $350 for our 24-tap operation).

On top of the collection equipment at the tree, you'll also need to acquire a storage container to hold the collected sap until it's time to boil. As an example, a 65-gallon plastic storage tank with threaded discharge valve will cost about $200. A much more reasonably priced alternative is to fit a plastic faucet (hose bib) onto a 35-gallon plastic garbage can. The garbage can and faucet setup will cost roughly $23. With either choice, it's critical to raise the units on some cinder blocks, so that you can slip a bucket underneath to draw off the sap when it's time to boil. But either way, it's an additional expense you'll incur, and keep in mind that you still won't have produced a single ounce of syrup yet. Aside from the cost, I want to share some thoughts about the drawbacks of using buckets.

USING BUCKETS:

- Neither type of bucket (plastic or metal) will prevent ants from entering and drowning in the sap.

- The arched lid on the traditional metal buckets allows rainwater, windblown debris and flies to enter and collect in the maple sap.

- When filled, both plastic and metal buckets are heavy enough to pull the tap out of the tree. When this happens the bucket falls to the ground and spills the contents.

- From a distance, you can't tell when a metal bucket is full. So someone will have to walk to each bucket and visually inspect them daily.

- You'll require extra empty buckets to re-hang while transferring the sap to your storage container.

- Over time, metal spiles, buckets and lids will begin to rust.

SAP BAGS

A relatively recent innovation in sap collection consists of 2-gallon plastic sap bags suspended from rustproof aluminum taps. The cost for 24 of each plus the metal bag hangers is around $225. This is more economical than plastic buckets, but sap bags have their share of shortcomings too.

USING SAP BAGS:

- The sap bag design won't keep the ants out either.

- If the sap freezes and expands, the plastic is somewhat prone to tearing.

- When filled above two-thirds of their capacity, the bags may burst.

- At season end, it's difficult to thoroughly dry the inside of the bags, inviting mildew formation to occur.

- You'll require extra empty bags to re-hang while transferring sap to your storage container.

- Sap bags have a relatively low acquisition cost, but bags only last a few seasons before they have to be replaced.

- Metal bag hangers will begin to rust over time.

- On the positive side, the 5/16 inch aluminum taps make a smaller tap hole, meaning at season end, the tree will heal faster.

- Aluminum taps won't rust.

PLASTIC MILK JUGS

During the early 1980s, another tapping system briefly came into vogue for backyard syrup makers. It involved cutting a hole into the shoulder of a 1-gallon plastic milk jug and hanging it on a metal spile. Based on 2011 prices, the total cost for a 24-tap operation using this collection system is slightly over $60. This is even more economical than the bag system, plus empty milk jugs are easy to accumulate (don't forget to keep the lids). The system was touted as a method for making syrup as inexpensively as possible, which is a fine idea, up to a point. However, after Paulie and I tried using plastic milk jugs to collect sap for ourselves, we quickly discovered that the system lacked utility for several reasons.

USING PLASTIC MILK JUGS:

- Ants will still find their way into your plastic milk jug sap containers.

- With a hole cut into the side, the plastic milk jug can only hold about three quarts before sap begins dripping out.

- You'll require extra empty milk jugs to re-hang while transferring sap to your storage container or you'll need more uncut empties to store your sap until you boil.

- Since milk jugs have very limited volume, they require almost constant monitoring and tending.

- Milk jugs can be hung from either ⁷⁄₁₆ inch steel spiles or ⁵⁄₁₆ inch aluminum taps.

- Since milk jugs are essentially weightless, on windy days empty jugs tend to blow off the spile, wasting sap while you're chasing them being blown down the road.

One common drawback to all of the collecting methods I've just outlined is that all of them involve transferring sap into some type of storage container. This means you've got to handle the sap more than once and I guarantee you'll spill some in the process (we always did).

5-GALLON PLASTIC JUGS

There's one more strategy I have found that a backyard sugar maker can adopt to solve the sap collection challenge. You see, after chasing milk jugs, picking dead ants out of buckets and expanding my lexicon of profanity from using bags, I finally hit upon a sap collection system that defeats the four enemies I referred to earlier — wind, weather, insects and a big time commitment. This strategy is inexpensive to acquire and assemble, saves time, eliminates the need for a storage tank and best of all — keeps those persistent ants out! I call it the "half n' half" method. It's a hybrid of the milk jug system and the tubing network. Before I get into how to do it, here's a little background information.

Years ago, while visiting a local fish and chips eatery, I noticed cases of empty cooking oil jugs piled by the dumpster, destined for recycling. Each held five gallons of oil and best of all — each had a screw-on plastic lid. The restaurant manager was more than willing to let me take them, even offering to save more for me. Jackpot! Eventually I collected about 50 of them. After pouring out the dregs of the frying oil and thoroughly washing each of them with scalding hot water and a degreaser, I dried them out completely. This was fairly easy to do, as each jug has a two inch threaded opening at the top. I'm pleased to say this resulted in not a bit of mildew.

Next, I acquired a 100-foot roll of plastic tubing, 24 plastic taps, "Y" connectors, "T" connectors and straight tubing connectors. Using 2011 prices, the whole outfit would still cost me less than $60, but keep in mind that I bought my supplies 17 years ago. I was also able to offset my costs by selling my old metal spiles,

> This strategy is inexpensive to acquire and assemble, saves time, eliminates the need for a storage tank and best of all — keeps those persistent ants out!

The total cost of a single plastic tap, "T" or "Y" connector and straight tubing connector is 60 percent less than a steel spile.

ASSEMBLING THE "HALF N' HALF" SAP COLLECTION SYSTEM

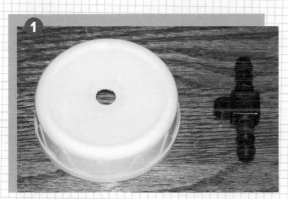

The drilled lid and straight tubing connector.

The lid and connector assembled plus the tubing and "Y" connector. The plastic tubing can be a bit stiff at times. To soften the ends before attaching it to the connectors, a quick dunk in some hot water helps.

The completed lower assembly.

The upper tubing lengths and taps — looking a little like a stethoscope.

buckets and lids to a large commercial "bucket" operation, so my actual out-of-pocket expense was probably less than $25. The next step was to assemble my "prototype."

After I removed the inner cap liner, I drilled a hole in the screw-on lid large enough to permit snapping a straight tubing connector into it, while still allowing the cap to spin freely. To that I added a short shot of tubing, connecting the other end to the bottom of a "Y" connector. To the upper ends of the "Y", I attached two more lengths of tubing and plastic taps on the ends of those.

When completed, my efforts yielded something resembling a doctor's stethoscope or plumber's nightmare! When it's time to tap, I drill two holes into the tree, insert the taps and start collecting. When a jug is filled with sap, I simply spin off the lid, screw it onto a clean empty jug and twist an un-drilled lid onto the filled jug. Upon testing my little homemade "half n' half" collection system, I found that it overcame many collection challenges.

Our homemade "half n' half" collection system fully deployed with two jugs and four taps adorning a massive sugar maple tree. No ants, no spillage and easy collection with this hybrid system.

THE BENEFITS OF USING THE "HALF N' HALF" SAP COLLECTION SYSTEM:

- Zip, zero, nada ants.

- The jugs sit on the ground, so they can't fall, tip or spill (unless the Law of Gravity is repealed).

- There is no chance of a full container pulling a tap out of the tree.

- When sealed with un-drilled lids, my filled jugs are my storage containers.

- Dishwasher cleanup of taps and connectors is a breeze (hot water wash, no detergent needed).

- The translucent plastic makes monitoring the jugs a snap, even from a distance.

- The five gallon volume means less time spent tending or replacing jugs.

- The larger volume collection permits one jug to service two taps.

- This system has extremely low acquisition costs.

- Swapping out a filled jug with a fresh empty takes about ten seconds and not one drop of sap is spilled.

- Replacement 5-gallon jugs and lids are readily available at no cost, all you have to do is ask around at commercial kitchens.

- The plastic taps and connectors will never rust.

So there you have it, our homemade "half n' half" collection system significantly reduced acquisition cost, increased efficiency and we had no ants to contend with. I only wish it hadn't taken me years to discover how relatively easy sap collection could be this way.

If there is a drawback in using this system it's that a filled 5-gallon cooking oil jug weighs about 43 pounds, lending new meaning to the term "heavy lifting." But, there is one more sap collection strategy that might work for you as well.

. . . .

4-GALLON PLASTIC JUGS

An equally inexpensive alternative to collecting sap in 5-gallon cooking oil jugs is to use 4-gallon drinking water bottles instead. Made of clear plastic and topped with a snap on lid, these containers possess many of the same positive attributes as the cooking oil jugs.

USING 4-GALLON PLASTIC JUGS:

- Sap volume can be visually monitored from long distances away.

- 4-gallon water bottles are free for the asking.

- The filled bottle, topped with an un-drilled cap transforms into a 4-gallon sap storage container.

- Since it was previously filled with potable water, it won't need to be degreased prior to deployment.

- The slightly lower volume translates into nine pounds less weight than the 5-gallon size when filled to capacity (about thirty-five pounds).

Sap collecting in a 5-gallon plastic cooking oil jug or 4-gallon clear plastic water bottle — you decide which works best for your system. Both are free for the asking.

- If the plastic becomes brittle or discolored, simply send it on to the recycling center and acquire a replacement. Many folks use water bottles this size in their home drinking water dispensers.

Sadly, when compared to the 5-gallon cooking oil jugs, there are a few minor drawbacks I have found for the 4-gallon water bottles.

DRAWBACKS OF USING THE 4-GALLON PLASTIC JUG:

- Since the jug is clear, it permits more UV and sunlight penetration, meaning your sap may spoil slightly faster.

- Each 4-gallon plastic jug holds twenty percent less than a 5-gallon cooking oil jug, so more containers are needed.

- Since many water bottles are round, as opposed to being square or rectangular and having flat sides, storing them in the off season might be a bit more problematic.

- Unlike the cooking oil jug, some water bottles lack a carrying handle.

But let's not dwell on the negative. The point is that you now have a second quite viable sap collection container that may prove just as useful to you as the larger cooking oil jug size. And best of all, it's free for the asking too. And there is no reason why you couldn't employ a mix n' match system using several of each (your maple trees will never know the difference).

TAPS

When selecting taps, you have essentially two basic choices, metal or plastic. If purchased by the dozen, classic galvanized steel or stainless spiles will cost about $2.50 each. You can choose between either 7/16 inch spiles or the 5/16 inch aluminum taps used with sap bagging systems. For plastic taps, you also have two options, either the 7/16 inch diameter or the newer, smaller style, the 5/16 inch diameter models. Both work well, and some research indicates that the smaller plastic models do not deter sap flow and actually help the tap holes heal

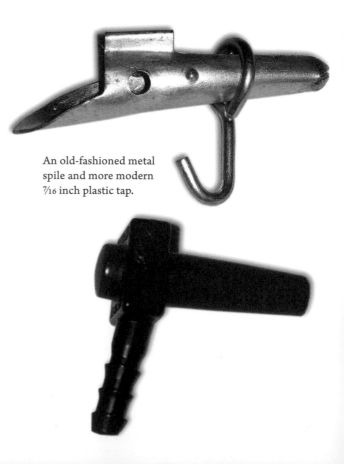

An old-fashioned metal spile and more modern 7/16 inch plastic tap.

faster at the end of the season. If they had been available in 1995, I'd have purchased smaller diameter taps myself. But perhaps the best advantage from a cost standpoint is that the combined cost of a plastic tap, "T" or "Y" connector and straight connector is less than half the cost of a single metal spile.

Installing a classic metal spile.

Sap weighs roughly nine pounds per gallon. Remember, your overall objective is to make maple syrup; it's not to damage your spine and strain your muscles in the process.

STORAGE CONTAINERS

I'd like to share one final note about sap storage containers. Sap weighs roughly nine pounds per gallon. Translated, this means a filled 65-gallon storage tank will tip the scales at nearly 600 pounds, and using a 35-gallon trash can version will weigh in at 315 pounds — roughly half that amount. So give some serious consideration as to what you'll store your sap in. Either alternative will be exceedingly difficult to relocate once you start filling it with sap — even if you have a strong sugaring partner to lend a hand. Remember, your overall objective is to make maple syrup; it's not to damage your spine and strain your muscles in the process.

CHAPTER 7

TAPPING TOOLS, TECHNIQUES & TIPS

· ·

WHEN "SUGAR TIME" arrives in your part of the country, there's plenty of work to be done before you can get down to boiling. Most of the tasks aren't difficult; merely time consuming, especially if a deep layer of snow still remains on the ground. So when the calendar says it's time to tap and you go looking for your tool belt, here are some suggestions of what to carry with you as you head out to the trees.

TAPPING TOOLS

SAP AUGER

Traditional sugar makers bore their tap holes using an auger bit like the one in the next photo. Equipped with a coarse screw point, an auger digs in quickly, boring a uniform smooth sided hole. The size you use will be governed by the diameter of your taps, either $7/16$ or $5/16$ inches. And make no mistake; an auger is an expensive tool. I paid $10 for mine in 1991 and shudder when I think about what the replacement cost for it would be today. But don't skimp when purchasing an auger. Paying a little more for a higher quality tool is well worth it. Look for one manufactured from high

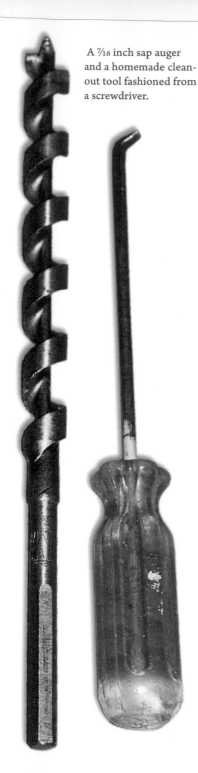

A 7/16 inch sap auger and a homemade clean-out tool fashioned from a screwdriver.

quality tool steel (U.S. or German made) that's razor sharp. The last thing you need is for the shank to snap off inside the hole, because it may be impossible to extract. After tapping is finished, clean your auger by wiping it down with a liberal coating of vegetable oil. Then wrap it in a clean rag and store it in a dry place. Never coat the tool with a petroleum-based lubricant. There are two other prohibitions that I will share with you, do not use your sap auger for any purpose other than tapping, and never loan it out unless you go with it.

DRILL

You've got two basic choices for drilling devices. I use a cordless electric drill. It works great and I'm not tethered to a mile of extension cord. If you prefer, an old-style carpenter's brace (drill) works fine too. As an example, Amish sugar makers have been boring tap holes with hand braces for centuries. To leverage gravity, drill your tap holes on a slightly upward angle as you drill into the tree. The hole should be 1 to 1½ inches deep, slightly deeper than the length of the tap. This encourages sap to pool up at the rear end of the hole creating a steadier flow.

CLEAN-OUT TOOL

After the tap hole is bored and the auger is withdrawn, sap may begin dripping out almost immediately, which is terrific. However, it's not time to insert the tap yet. You must first clean out the hole to remove any loose bits of wood. I fashioned my clean-out tool from an old slotted screwdriver by heating the tip prior to bending it 90 degrees. I've never found factory-made clean-out tools for sale anywhere — it's strictly a homemade appliance. But if you can't abide the thought of destroying a screwdriver, you can fashion a clean-out tool using a large nail. I was forced to undertake this one year myself, when I foolishly misplaced my regular tool. Using my vise and a heavy file, I bent and shaped a substitute in about 5 minutes.

HAMMER

A standard claw hammer is an essential tapping tool, particularly if you're tapping older sugar maples trees with thick layers of outer bark. Use the claw end to gently pry away a small section of the dead outer surface before drilling your tap hole. After you drill the hole and insert the tap, rap it gently to ensure it won't slip out. The key here is not to be aggressive. If you whack it too hard you'll split the inner bark. This will injure the tree and you'll have a leaky hole that wastes sap while at the same time attracting many ants and flies. If you are setting a plastic tap, tunk it (or thump if you prefer) sharply but gently with the side of the hammer. Then give it a gentle test tug. If the tap resists pulling out, you can move on to the

A properly installed plastic tap. Remember, *tunk* it, don't smack it with the hammer.

next tree. If the tap still seems a bit loose, tunk it once more to seat it securely.

With metal taps, there is a metal tab on the top specifically designed to be struck with a hammer. But once again, tap it in gently so as not to damage the tree.

Using our 24-tap operation as a yardstick, my total tapping time, which also includes installing the sap containers, will take about two hours. Good luck in your endeavors. You're now one step closer to enjoying you own homemade maple syrup.

TAPPING TIPS

To maximize sap flow, initially tap your trees on the southern side. Early in the season, this ensures maximum exposure to the sun's rays which will increase sap flow. Later on, provided the tree is large enough, you may wish to add a tap on the north side as well, prolonging the sap flow. You'll get more sap if you install your taps directly beneath larger branches. Tap as close to the soil line as your collection system (bucket and jug height) will permit. The closer your tap is to the roots, the more sap you will divert into your collection containers. A 16-inch diameter tree can safely accommodate one tap, a 20-inch diameter tree can handle two taps and a 36-inch diameter tree can handle three taps without any attendant damage.

Tap your trees on a bright, sunny day. Even if the air temperature is slightly below freezing, sap will likely be running if the sun is shining. As you withdraw the auger, sap may begin dripping out almost immediately. After you clean out the hole, catch a few drops on your finger and have a taste. You should be able to detect a subtle "sweet" taste even in the raw sap. Go ahead and try some, you certainly won't be the first anxious rookie sugar maker to do so — or the last!

If you have young children, "helping" mom or dad tap the trees is a reasonably safe activity they can participate in along with your supervision, so enjoy tapping time as a family activity. Please take note, boiling and many of the

> To maximize sap flow, initially tap your trees on the southern side. Later on, if the tree is large enough, add a tap on the north side as well, prolonging the sap flow.

other tasks involved in making maple syrup are obviously too dangerous for young kids. If your children are young teens, that's a different matter altogether. But if your kids are 8-years-old or younger, tapping should be the only task they help with, at least until after the first batch of syrup is finally finished. Test tasting some freshly made "Jack Wax" (see Additional Resources at the back of the book for the "recipe") of maple syrup on crushed ice is definitely a family oriented activity youngsters will enjoy. The point here is to introduce making maple syrup as a family tradition. As your sugaring skills improve, it will be your responsibility and hopefully your pleasure to pass onto your kids everything your years of maple sugaring experience have taught you.

IF YOU HAVE YOUNG CHILDREN, "HELPING" MOM OR DAD TAP THE TREES IS A REASONABLY SAFE ACTIVITY THEY CAN PARTICIPATE IN ALONG WITH YOUR SUPERVISION.

CHAPTER 8

COLD SEPARATION 101

. . . .

A s I DISCUSSED in Chapter 1, making maple syrup involves processing raw sap to get rid of everything that isn't syrup — meaning about 97 percent of the volume which is the average water content of sugar maple sap. For a small-scale producer like me (or you), that translates into endless hours of outdoor boiling. And how much end product will result? Well, if I'm lucky and weather conditions are perfect, boiling 45 to 50 gallons of raw sap might yield five quarts of syrup. Depending upon your perspective, it's either a labor of love or a fool's errand. Fortunately, there's a nifty strategy backyard syrup makers can employ which will either shorten boiling times and reduce fuel use or increase the yield. In educational parlance, either scenario results in "significantly enhanced outcomes." But before I get started, let's review some basic high school chemistry.

Sap left outside overnight during freezing temperatures offers an easy way to remove up to 25% of the water present using cold separation.

> Making maple syrup involves processing raw sap to get rid of everything that isn't syrup — meaning about 97 percent of the volume.

PHYSICAL VS. CHEMICAL REACTIONS

Outside of particle bombardment using an "atom-smasher," compounds may be subjected to two basic types of processes, either chemical or physical. As an example, boiling is a physical process — an accelerated form of evaporation. The water in boiling sap vaporizes into steam and floats away. And in doing this there is no chemical change to the water molecules. They are simply rendered into a different physical state. So here's a thought, what if you could begin making syrup and get rid of some of the water without boiling? Well you can, it's called cold separation, which is a fancy term for freezing.

YOU COULD BEGIN MAKING SYRUP AND GET RID OF SOME OF THE WATER WITHOUT BOILING. IT'S CALLED COLD SEPARATION, WHICH IS A FANCY TERM FOR FREEZING.

FREEZING OUT THE WATER

During the crisp starlit nights that occur regularly during prime sugaring weather, for us, evening temperatures frequently drop into the low-20° F range. If left outside in an exposed location, our sap containers begin forming a layer of ice around their interior walls, while the now concentrated liquefied sugar/sap migrates to a central cavity that forms in the vessel. A resourceful sugar maker can drain this liquid into an empty container and reduce boiling times correspondingly. If luck is on your side, and the temperature drops into the high teens, you may be able to sequester and remove as much as 25 percent of the water, saving precious wood and significantly reducing the overall boiling time.

I discovered this fantastic phenomenon by accident, and immediately upon tasting a sample of the sap in my frozen jugs, realized I was onto something important. If the early spring weather continues to cooperate with warm sunny days and frosty nights, you might even freeze additional water out of the concentrated sap. But before you can undertake a second freeze-off, you've got to transfer the concentrate into another container. Here is the method I've developed.

I acquired a food-grade plastic bucket from our local horseradish factory and used my 1-inch spade bit to cut a hole in the side, just above the bottom. Then I installed a plastic valve, securing it on the inside with a gasket and retaining nut. On the end of the spout, I slipped on a shot of plastic tubing and it was ready to go. Valves of this type can be purchased at many hardware or home improvement stores. Expect to pay about four dollars for this retrofit. Here is a photo of the setup in use.

To transfer the sap concentrate, I bust a hole in the center of the icy contents of one of my 5-gallon storage jugs, tip it into the bucket and gravity does most of the work, draining the concentrate into an empty storage jug. If any small chunks of ice end up floating in the bucket, it's a simple matter to skim them out using an ordinary kitchen strainer. I've put 1 gallon graduation marks along the outside of the transfer bucket allowing me to better gauge how much water has been frozen out. As I mentioned before, that usually works out to around twenty-five percent, which is a big deal for me, and could be for you as well.

Under ideal boiling conditions, meaning low barometric pressure and reasonably warm air, my small evaporator will boil off about six gallons of sap per hour. On a typical 45 to 50 gallon boil, cold separating either reduces outdoor boiling time by about two hours, or if I boil 45 to 50 gallons of concentrated sap, increases my yield

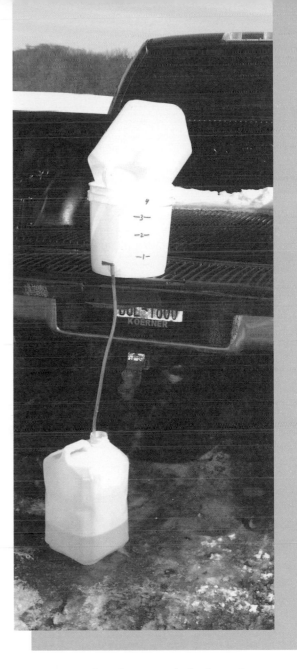

Concentrated sap drains into the bucket and down into a fresh storage container with no spills. Graduation marks can be seen on the transfer rig.

by about three pints. If the night before I boil has been frosty cold, I frequently drain the bucket of concentrate directly into the pre-heater on my evaporator. It saves time and reduces footwork.

COLD SEPARATION

Cold separating is the nearly exclusive domain of amateur sugar makers. Larger commercial operations, if they can afford one, employ a reverse osmosis "RO" machine to remove water from raw sap. An RO machine is capable of removing about 50 percent of the water and will process as much as 7,500 gallons of sap per day. The units are brutally expensive, but since a large sugaring operation might collect that much sap in a single day, the fuel savings, coupled with the reduced boiling times, offers a positive payback. But with my ragtag little setup of 24 taps, the cost of an RO unit is prohibitive. However on the positive side, frigid night air is free!

There is one other significant advantage to be garnered from cold separating; the technique helps eliminate nitre. The mineral salts that make up nitre are dissolved in the water portion of the sap, so freezing out some percentage of the water "traps" those compounds in the ice. You won't be saddled with the task of filtering them out, because they won't be in your concentrated sap to begin with.

My somewhat unique cold separation technique also highlights a glaring short-

> If I'm lucky and weather conditions are perfect, boiling 45 to 50 gallons of raw sap might yield 5 quarts of syrup.

coming of storing sap in a single large tank or a plastic garbage can — namely you will require another storage container to drain the concentrated sap into. It also presupposes that the tank or can has been sufficiently elevated to allow that second container to be positioned below it. If either is completely filled, it will be too heavy to lift and move, even if your sugaring partner is a former NFL lineman!

There's another problem you'll have to confront as well — the weight of the remaining ice. Let's assume for a moment that you did manage to drain your 65-gallon storage tank into another container, and let's also assume that you froze out fifteen percent of the water — roughly ten gallons. At that point, your tank still has almost ninety pounds of ice inside which will need to be removed prior to storing any more sap. It's going to take a river of hot water to melt that ice, adding extra legwork, time and expense to your syruping efforts.

All of these inconveniences should point out the benefit of storing sap in 5-gallon jugs or 4-gallon drinking water containers. Not only are both items free for the asking, each is of a manageable size and weight. Admittedly, 45 pounds is still heavy, but one person still can lift it — 600 pounds one person cannot lift.

Not to add insult to injury, but if you hang 24 taps as I do, you'll probably need more than one large sap storage container — another additional expense for your sugaring efforts.

One final note, if the notion of visiting a horseradish factory starts to make you woozy thinking of the strong vapors, food-grade plastic buckets may also be acquired from practically any restaurant supply company.

A plastic draw-off valve with threaded stem, "O" ring seal and threaded retaining nut used for the transfer bucket.

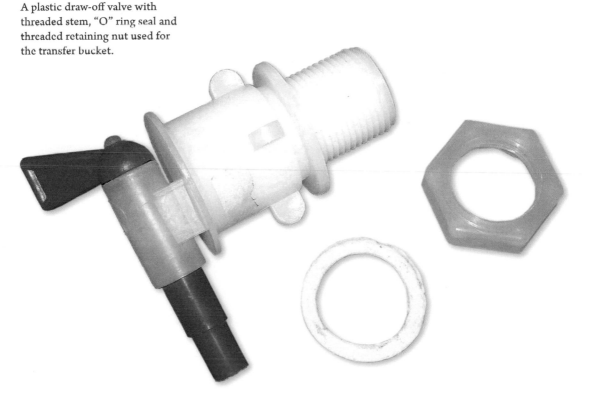

THE TRIALS OF USING A 35-GALLON GARBAGE CAN FOR STORAGE

///

> Just like my original washtub evaporator, I've kept that garbage can as a constant reminder of another practice *not* to employ.

IN THE SPIRIT of full disclosure, Paulie and I *did* experiment with storing sap in a 35-gallon plastic garbage can. We fitted the container with a plastic hose bib (faucet) and elevated the unit on several rows of cinder blocks. To offset the problem with ice building up around the inside, we fitted the rear of the hose bib with a threaded connector and an L-shaped section of PVC pipe which extended upward toward the center where the concentrated sap remained liquefied, thus keeping the hose bib from freezing. (The PVC pipe, elbow and threaded connector cost about $3.50 at 2012 prices. The hose bib I already had). Until we wised up we had to deal with two problems. First, on a particularly bitter night, about 30 percent of the sap froze and expanded. In doing so it caused the lid to tear. Scratch one lid. We were then forced to cover the garbage can with a piece of plywood weighted with another cinder block. The second problem was that while we froze out a significant amount of water, as previously stated, we ended up with nearly 90 pounds of ice which needed to be melted out before we could resume using the garbage can.

Just like my original washtub evaporator, I've kept that garbage can as a constant reminder of another practice *not* to employ. For Paulie and I, sugaring off involved a good deal of trial and error. We were judged at many trials, because we committed so many errors. This episode was simply one more in a long string of them.

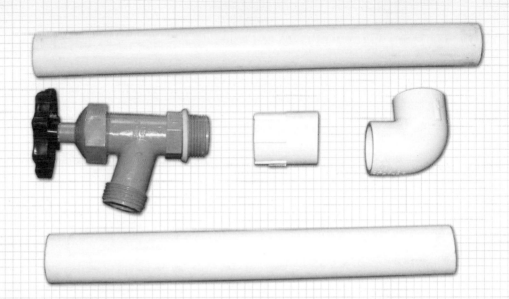

THE PITFALLS OF STORING SAP
IN A 35-GALLON GARBAGE CAN:

- Completely filled, the unit will weigh nearly 325 pounds making it difficult if not impossible to move. Worse yet, the weight limit on our garbage can was 200 pounds. Had we even *tried* to lift it, we'd have likely torn the handles off, dropped the garbage can, and lost most of our concentrated sap.

- If the garbage can is filled to capacity, the expanding sap on a bitter cold night may destroy the cover or worse yet cause the garbage can itself to rupture.

- Melting out as much as 90 pounds of ice will wreak havoc with your utility bill adding additional expense to your sugaring efforts.

- Counting the cost of the garbage can and hose bib rig, you'll be investing an additional $30 to store your sap.

Above: Hose bib and PVC components for use with a 35-gallon garbage can sap storing system. *Right:* Assembled components.

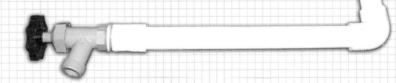

CHAPTER 9

KEEP IT COLD & KEEP IT CLEAR

N CHAPTER 8, I explained the advantages and techniques involved in doing cold separation. If executed properly, freezing out the water instead of boiling it out can significantly reduce the time needed to complete a batch of syrup. But it's important to remember that freezing out that pesky water is done on frosty, cold nights, when your storage containers have been left out in an exposed location to get extra cold.

SAP MUST BE STORED WHERE IT RECEIVES MINIMAL EXPOSURE TO BOTH HEAT AND LIGHT.

During sunny, daylight hours in the late winter or early spring "mud season" when temperatures might climb up to 50 F, sap must be stored where it receives minimal exposure to both heat and light. This is because of bacterial contamination. Depending upon which method you use for your sap collection, the sap may have already begun to play host to some native airborne yeast organisms or other forms of microscopic guests. Surprisingly, there are some types of bacteria living in maple sap even when it's still inside the tree.

This 140-year-old sugar maple in the author's front yard is about 5 feet in diameter. Nicknamed Ernie, it is a bonafide "six-holer."

BACTERIA WOES

If your sap gets warm, it can be the perfect home for bacteria — a warm, moist location with plenty of food, or sugar, for them to feast upon. So at a minimum, you've got to keep your stored sap cold. It's a pretty straightforward task. There's usually plenty of snow around, so all you have to do is bunker it up into a heavy layer to keep it cold.

To do this, chop out a cavity in a snow bank that is in a naturally shaded part of your property. Stand the container(s) in the bottom of the snow cave and bury them under the snow. That's all there is to it. The more snow you can pile on top and the shadier the location you select, the longer your sap will last without spoiling. The length will vary and could be as long as three weeks. I have used this technique successfully many, many times.

During March 1993, upstate New York was struck by a savage blizzard that dumped fifty-two inches of snow during one single night! Luckily, the day before I'd collected fifteen gallons of sap and had set the containers on top of the existing snow in the yard. After the blizzard, the snow was so deep I couldn't even see where my jugs were buried. But I didn't need to worry, three weeks later when the blizzard snow pack finally started to recede and began to disappear; I found my jugs and the sap was still crystal clear. Had the sap spoiled, it would have taken on a milky, cloudy appearance which would have made it unfit for boiling.

As it turned out, the syrup that we made from that sap won a Second Premium (red ribbon) at the 1993 New York State Fair. So keep your sap cold and covered, and it will stay fresh.

> If your sap gets warm, it can be the perfect home for bacteria — a warm, moist location with plenty of food for them to feast upon.

Properly bunkered up in snow and stored in a shady location, sap will keep for weeks without spoiling.

CHAPTER 10

GETTING DOWN TO BOILING

· ·

N OW THAT YOU'VE collected a sufficient quantity of sap and perhaps did some cold separating to help the water removal process along, it's time to begin boiling. After your fire is roaring, set your evaporator atop the arch and fill it with two to three inches of raw sap. As it starts to bubble and steam, frothy white foam will begin to accumulate on the surface. This is the first of the nitre. To remove it, simply skim it off with a skimming tool or a kitchen strainer. Rinse your skimmer in a bucket of water after use and repeat the skimming process whenever it is needed.

I've skimmed with a round kitchen strainer, but if you are using a sectioned rectangular evaporator, the rectangular shape will allow you to skim more efficiently and get right to the edges and corners also.

A skimming tool makes removing nitre a breeze. Notice that at the beginning of the process, boiling sap looks exactly like boiling water.

BOILING AND THE EVAPORATOR PAN

If you're boiling your sap in an open container such as a washtub, try to keep it as level as possible. If you are using a proper evaporator with a sectioned or "chambered" pan like mine, you must make sure that you level it from front to back and side to side. This is not optional; it's an absolute requirement. When raw sap is fed into the first chamber, it will "push" the more sugar-laden portion of the liquid to the leftmost chamber. This occurs because of the different densities that raw sap has as it gets partially cooked down. It's a natural phenomenon that is supposed to occur, but if your evaporator isn't level, this won't happen. To level my evaporator, I laid a small magnetic torpedo level on the pan and shimmed the wheels with thin pieces of scrap wood. Obviously, the time to do this is before you fire up the unit and add raw sap to the evaporator pan.

As you begin boiling, initially the sap will look exactly like boiling water, and remember, 97 percent of it is just water. However, in a few hours the boiling mixture will begin to show its first signs of "color." This is a positive sign, because it indicates that the sugar content is slowly beginning to rise. If you take a few sniffs of the rising steam, it's possible you may even detect the faint smell of maple — another positive development. Just keep stoking the fire. Inside the arch, you will want a blaze reminiscent of that famous one they had in Chicago years ago!

As you boil your sap, the level in the evaporator will begin to drop and you'll need to replenish it with fresh raw sap. If the refilling sap is at an ice cold temperature going in, it will quite likely lower the temperature so much that it kills the boil — costing you valuable time until the temperature comes back up high enough. There's a simple solution to this dilemma, and for that you will need to fashion a reservoir or pre-heater to your evaporator.

Photographed through the rising steam, and taken about three hours after the skimming picture, the boiling sap is beginning to show faint signs of "color." This is about halfway through a day's boiling. The sap is now amber colored. A copper feed line connects to the pre-heater reservoir.

PRE-HEATER

My small evaporator is equipped with a six gallon reservoir or pre-heater sporting a bronze gate valve connected to a copper feed line. The rising steam from my evaporator preheats the sap inside this reservoir. As the liquid level in the evaporator drops, I can open the valve to let a constant trickle of raw sap enter the evaporator. With this setup, the boil doesn't stop.

In looking back to that first year when Paulie and I boiled using a washtub, we fashioned a rudimentary pre-heater using a 3-pound coffee can. Near the bottom we punctured the can with a nail. Then we laid a plank across the top of the washtub, set the coffee can on top of it and filled the can with sap. The hole permitted a small but steady stream of sap to be continually added to the evaporator below without killing the boil. We used a metal coffee can, but a plastic one would work just as well.

A word of caution though — do not set your pre-heater on a pressure treated plank. The rising steam will condense onto the plank and some of the toxic preservative in the wood may begin dripping into your evaporator.

BOIL YOUR OLDEST SAP FIRST AND PROGRESSIVELY WORK YOUR WAY THROUGH TO THE FRESHEST SAP.

THE BOILING PROCESS

As boiling continues and you progressively add fresh sap, the color of the boiling liquid will gradually turn a darker color indicating that the sugar content is rising. To some extent, you can control this color transition by not agitating the surface of the boiling sap with overly aggressive skimming. Splashing sap onto the uncovered surface of your evaporator will cause the sugar to caramelize. The other contributing factor to syrup color is the reaction of the natural amino acids in the sap when they are exposed to the heat of the fire. The concentration of these amino acids increases as you progress farther into the season. This means the earlier you can boil, the better your chances of producing a lighter colored syrup. There is much more about syrup grading covered in Chapter 11.

Here are few other considerations to think about with the boiling process. First, boil your oldest sap first and progressively work your way through to the freshest sap. Properly chilled in a bunker of deep

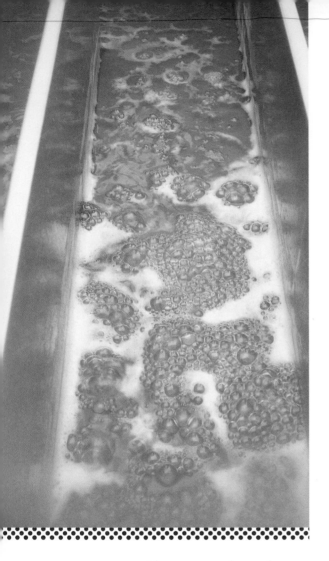

After seven more hours of boiling, the "sugar boil" has pockets of glossy of bubbles surrounded by floating ribbons of nitre. When your sap begins to look like this, it's time to head to the kitchen and continue the finishing work indoors.

snow, sap will remain fresh for two to three weeks, but it will eventually begin to get cloudy as the bacteria present in the sap reproduce, contaminating your sap. So always use the oldest sap first.

Secondly, if weather permits you to do this, try to boil on a day with falling barometric pressure. The sap will actually boil at a slightly lower temperature under these conditions and will boil more aggressively as well.

Next, based upon the surface area of your evaporator, you may need to begin boiling while it's still dark and spend many hours tending the fire and your rig. As an example, for a 45- to 50-gallon boil in mid-March, I usually fire up my arch about 4 o'clock in the morning. Maintaining a roaring blaze is critical, and you're liable to get a bit tired and probably in need of refreshment. For this reason, I'd recommend finding a sugaring partner to help with the work. I'd also recommend cooling a few bottles of liquid refreshment into the snow in case a bad case of the "thirsty's" happens to appear.

Once the last of your sap has been added to the evaporator, it's time to begin monitoring the temperature. It will slowly begin rising past the boiling point of water (212° F). When the temperature reaches about 215° F, it's time to prepare for the next phase — finishing. To give you better control, I'd suggest transferring the remaining liquid into some kitchen stock pots and moving the production indoors. As a process, finishing is much easier done in the relatively controlled environment of your kitchen.

Lastly, as the end of the outdoor boiling time approaches; be mindful not to let the fire become too hot, or the sap may develop a rolling boil and begin rising. This will cause excessive caramelizing. If this does occur, don't panic! Simply toss in a few bits of fresh clean snow. This will knock the rolling boil back down to a tamer level. This is also another sign that it's probably time to empty the evaporator and head for the kitchen.

BOILING TIPS

When I give presentations about making maple syrup at home, I'm invariably asked if it's possible to accomplish the entire process of cooking down the sap on the kitchen stove. And my answer to this question is always a resounding, "No!" The reason being is that your stove can't generate enough heat to boil the sap rapidly enough and on top of that, you'll wreck havoc with your utility bill. In addition, pots, even if they are large stock pots, have a relatively small surface area when compared to the area of an evaporator pan. If you boil on an open wood fire, the blaze will cook sap at 500-600° F — far hotter than the burner on a kitchen range. If you boil on an evaporator rig that has a fire brick-lined arch, you might be boiling at temperatures as high as 800° F. How hot is that? Well, at 800 degrees a piece of steel will glow cherry red, exactly the color the grate

> I'm invariably asked if it's possible to accomplish the entire process of cooking down the sap on the kitchen stove. And my answer to this question is always a resounding, "No!"

in my arch develops. But most significantly, my evaporator pan has a surface area of 5.3 square feet, which accounts for the six gallons per hour boiling rate.

In addition to enriching the power company, there's one more glaring reason not to perform 100 percent of your boiling in the kitchen — and that is the excess steam. If your kitchen is wallpapered, the decorative paper will have peeled off the wall and fallen to the floor long before you have finished making maple syrup.

Another factor to keep in mind is your comfort and the weather. As a backyard boiler you may be starting before the sun rises and while temperatures remain below freezing. Dress appropriately and in multiple layers. Wear old clothes if you can. Boiling sap was never intended to be a fashion statement. Most likely, by the time you head inside to do the finishing phase, your garments will reek of wood smoke and will be adorned with soot stains and dirt. So there's no point in ruining your best flannel shirts. Also keep in mind that by mid-afternoon the temperature may have risen by 30 degrees or more. With multiple layers you can begin shedding them as needed when the mercury rises.

POST-BOIL CLEANUP

There's one last item to that I want to cover here, the post-boil cleanup. Whether you are using a proper evaporator pan or a humble washtub, it must be scrubbed before you can boil in it again. While one person lugs the stock pots back to the kitchen, the other should place the empty boiling pan back over the fire and immediately fill it with water. Use the remaining heat below to warm this water. While it's warming, scrub out the accumulated nitre and caramelized sugar residue with a plastic scouring pad or long-handled brush. When the deposits have been scrubbed free, remove the pan, dump the water and allow the fire to begin burning itself out. Remember, the more residual sap you remove after this first boil, the less nitre you'll filter during the next step.

The critical thing to remember is to draw the water ahead of time and dump it into the evaporator as soon as the sap is moved into the stock pots for the trip indoors. If you do not, the heat will buckle the metal, melt the welds and your evaporator will soon resemble a pile of scrap metal! So you've got to move fast.

While you're still attending to outside chores, pick up any unburned wood and get it under cover. Then it's time to head inside and begin the next phase, the process of finishing.

Properly leveled and fired up, my evaporator is already hard at work.

CHAPTER 11

FINISHING, FILTERING & GRADING

You may be surprised at how long it takes for the thermometer to reach 218° F. But when it does, it's time to get busy.

THE FINISHING PROCESS involves carefully boiling the liquid that was drawn off of the evaporator and brought into your kitchen (or other closed environment). If the liquid that was boiled outside had reached 215° F (102 C), it's on the way to becoming syrup, but it's not quite maple syrup yet. So put your stock pot(s) on the stove and continue the boiling. If you initially had eight to ten quarts of liquid at the beginning of this step, its volume will further decrease as the boiling continues. During the ensuing hours (yes, hours!), you must closely monitor the temperature. You may be surprised at how long it takes for the thermometer to reach 218° F (103 C). But when it does, it's time to get busy.

After reaching 218° F it is time to filter your "syrup" for the first time. I always use a pair of Dacron cloth filters nested one inside the other and set them into a long-handled jelly strainer. But before you beginning to filter, skim off any floating sugar sand (nitre) from the surface, and reduce the heat slightly.

FILTERING THE NITRE

- Thoroughly wet the filters in the hottest water you can stand and squeeze (don't wring) out the excess.

- Nest the filters inside the strainer.

- Using a large ladle, add seven or eight ladles of liquid to the filter cone and let it drain into a clean pot.

- Immediately return the new pot to the stove for additional heating.

- Clean the filters by turning them inside out and rinsing them in hot water.

- Repeat with smaller quantities of liquid each time.

FILTERING & CLEANUP

For the first round of filtering, dump seven or eight ladles of liquid into the filters and let it drain through. The filters will trap some of the nitre that you must wash from the filters each round and before you can continue. Each time you fill the filters, add progressively less liquid. This is because more nitre crystals will be scooped out each time. Just keep at it until the stock pot is fully drained. Most likely, there will be a cooked-on layer of nitre coating the bottom of the pot. A vigorous scrubbing using clean, hot water will dissolve this quite quickly.

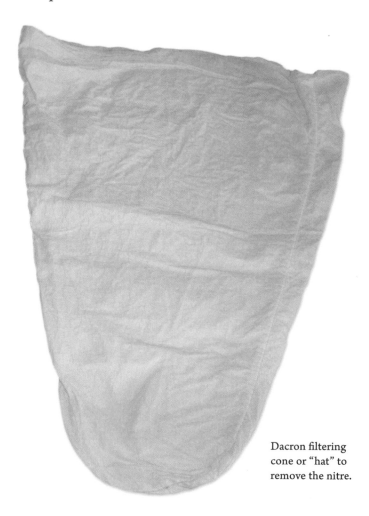

Dacron filtering cone or "hat" to remove the nitre.

In 1994, Paulie and I purchased a proper maple syrup raw wool filtering cone and set one of our Dacron filters inside it. Neither of us noticed any improvement in the amount of nitre this arrangement removed, but we did discover two unpleasant consequences. First, we ended up with a small amount of lint floating in our once filtered liquid, and after washing the wool filter in cold water and air drying it — it shrank. I keep it as a reminder that old technology is not necessarily the best technology, much like collecting sap in metal buckets with hinged lids versus the new innovations.

> Regardless of which filtering media you use, the entire process is more easily accomplished with two people, and this further underscores the value of making syrup with a partner.

But regardless of which filtering media you use, the entire process is more easily accomplished with two people, and this further underscores the value of making syrup with a partner. While one is busy cleaning the filters, the other can scrub the pot clean and fill it with tap water. You'll need that water for the next step, a sterilizing bath for your syrup containers. If you've got a second stock pot of "almost syrup" going, repeat the steps previously outlined. As the volume continues to decrease with continued boiling, you may be able to consolidate the two pots into one.

The initial filtering will eliminate a good portion of the sugar sand (nitre). If this is your first experience with filtering, don't be surprised that the inside of your Dacron filter will be coated with a kind of grungy residue.

SUGAR SAND

What exactly is this residue inside your filter? Called sugar sand (nitre), it consists of the various salts that were previously dissolved in the water portion of the sap. These are common mineral salts such as calcium chloride that precipitate out as the sugar content of the boiling sap increases. Hard water scale is composed of exactly these same types of compounds. Filtering out these impurities will eventually yield the crystal clear maple syrup you'll soon begin bottling or canning. These minerals aren't poisonous or dangerous, but if left in the syrup, they produce a bitter aftertaste that will rob the maple syrup of some of its sweetness — partially defeating the reason you're making this stuff to begin with.

Sugar sand (nitre) is nasty looking stuff.

Boiling at 218° F

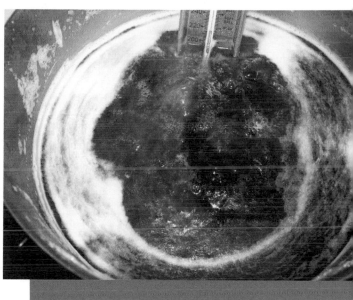

When the thermometer reaches 218° F, the nitre that is floating on top of the surface represents just the "tip of the iceberg." The heavier stuff is either suspended in the syrup or has fallen to the bottom of the pot. Just as if you were making jam, the easiest method to remove the floating crystals is to skim the surface with a large spoon. You'll waste very little syrup this way. After the first round of filtering you'll have clearer syrup — making an initial quick "eyeball" grading possible.

After the initial filtering is completed, continue boiling and monitoring the temperature. When the temperature climbs slightly above 220° F (105 C), you've got syrup. Repeat the filtering process again, draining the twice filtered liquid into another clean pot. If you want additional proof that you've got syrup, there are two ways to test this.

With the temperature now at 218° F, it's time for the first round of filtering. Remember to skim off the floating sugar sand (nitre) before you start. This batch, the first of the season eventually graded out at medium amber — which is exactly what I expected.

TESTING SUGAR LEVELS

If you're an absolute stickler for accuracy, you'll need to acquire a test cup and syrup hydrometer to measure the specific gravity of the liquid, which in this instance translates directly to show the sugar content. The hydrometer is graduated in the Baumé (pronounced bo-may) and brix degrees scales.

After the test cup is filled, stand the hydrometer in it. The unit will begin to float and depending on whether you are performing a "hot" test or a "cold" test, the red graduation marks will indicate if you've made syrup or not. The brix test measures the percentage of sugar that the liquid contains. Using these tests the syrup is ready when reading measure somewhere between 66 and 68 brix (% sugar solids) or 36 degrees Baumé. Readings above 68 brix indicate that you've reached a level of super saturation which may cause "maple rock" to form on the bottom of the container as the syrup cools.

All bona fide maple syrup, regardless of grade (more on this to follow) must have a sugar content of at least 67 percent and if you are finishing your batch at 220° F you'll be right on target.

To purchase a short test cup and syrup hydrometer expect to pay about $40. If this expense is not in your budget, there's an easier method. While not as reliable as the precise brix measurement, this technique has been used by backyard sugar makers for many years.

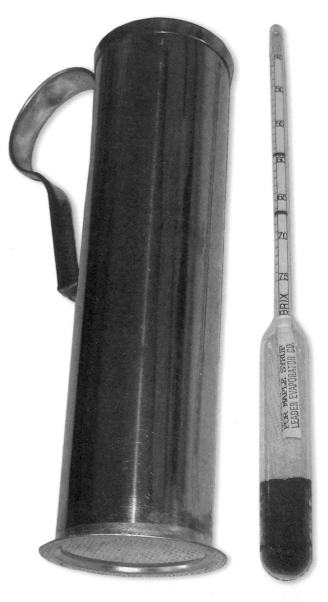

A test cup and hydrometer.

THE SPATULA TEST

Dip the blade of a wide spatula into the syrup and slowly withdraw it. If the liquid slowly sheets ("aprons") off the end, you've got syrup. When it cools a bit, you can swipe a finger across what's left and let your taste buds confirm what your eyes already know. I've used both methods. The spatula has one other advantage too. If you drop the spatula, it won't break. If you accidentally drop the fragile hydrometer, you won't be as fortunate and you can always buy a replacement for about $12 (ouch!).

A proper grading kit is a must-have for the serious backyard maple syrup producer.

GRADING MAPLE SYRUP

Now begins the fun part — the grading. This is when you'll find out exactly what kind of syrup you've made. And to do this accurately, you're going to need a grading kit.

The USDA has established four color-based grades of maple syrup: light amber, medium amber, dark amber, and grade B. The maple syrup grading kit contains four little bottles containing certified color samples plus an empty sample test bottle. Carefully fill the test bottle with your newly produced syrup and compare its color to the samples.

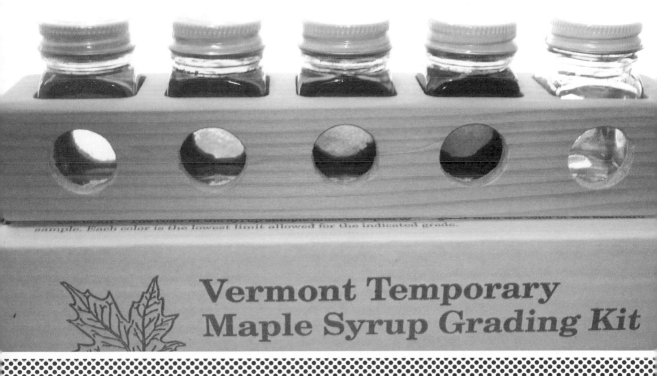

Vermont Temporary Maple Syrup Grading Kit

MAPLE SYRUP TERMINOLOGY

Vermont leads the United States in maple syrup production, boiling down roughly 50 percent of the total produced in the nation. As the leading producer organization, the Vermont Maple Sugar Makers' Association has its own ideas about maple terminology. For example, the association eschews the term "light amber" preferring to call it "fancy" grade instead. Additionally, the association uses the word "syrup" when referring to its principal maple product, as opposed to the USDA which chooses to spell it "sirup" in many of its official documents. Go figure! As the USDA does not actually produce any syrup, devoting its efforts instead to the copious generation of reports, studies and the like, I'll stick with the Vermonters when it comes to maple syrup nomenclature.

> MAPLE SYRUP IS ALSO A TERRIFIC SUBSTITUTE FOR SUGAR IN A STEAMING CUP OF EARL GREY TEA.

With a proper grading kit each of the four grades is progressively darker and will be increasingly more flavorful. Fancy grade is the lightest color and has the most delicate taste. Before commercially produced table sugar became widely available, fancy grade maple syrup was commonly used as a sweetener and baking ingredient. I have also found that maple syrup is also a terrific substitute for sugar in a steaming cup of Earl Grey tea. For syrup to be of a certain grade, it must be no darker than the certified color sample. As an example, if your syrup is darker than fancy, but lighter than medium amber, the syrup grades out as medium amber and so on. A word of warning though, please don't mistakenly take a swig of the color testing samples thinking they are syrup; they're actually a mixture of glycerin and burnt/raw umber (dirt).

GRADE B

One final note about syrup, you won't find any grade B for sale in stores. This is because it's sold in bulk — usually in 55-gallon drums. Likely you won't be slathering it on your French toast at home, but you have doubtless eaten some nonetheless. Grade B is sold to the processed food industry as a flavoring agent. It contributes the maple taste found in many brands of pancake syrup, maple cured ham and bacon, maple flavored frosting and maple walnut ice cream. So you've probably consumed more grade B syrup than you realize.

TO GRADE OR NOT TO GRADE

Provided you've filtered your syrup to remove all the nitre, grading is an optional task. However, if one of your goals is to enter some in a competitive judging at a maple festival, county or state fair, grading is imperative, because improperly graded entries suffer immediate disqualification.

If you're satisfied with the color and clarity of your syrup, then it's time to start bottling. And feel free to have a few tastes of your homemade nectar, believe me, you've earned it.

I like to pour my taste "tests" into a small glass and let it cool down a bit first before I savor the flavor.

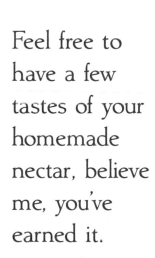

Feel free to have a few tastes of your homemade nectar, believe me, you've earned it.

CHAPTER 12

BOTTLING OR CANNING

CONGRATULATIONS, YOU HAVE completed finishing, filtering and grading your syrup. If you started with 45 to 50 gallons of sap to boil down, you've probably been at work for about 15 hours already, so you'll be glad to know you're almost finished. The only tasks left are to pour that golden, delicious syrup into a container and then cleaning up the inevitable spills. Even if you try to wipe up errant spills and drips while you're working, there will always be a few sticky spots that got missed. I'm fairly comfortable with the notion that anyone reading this book already knows how to scrub pots and mop floors. Most people consider the cleanup as a necessary evil that comes with the project and there's little chance of avoiding it.

TYPES OF CONTAINERS
- GLASS
- PLASTIC
- METAL

CHOOSING CONTAINERS

There are however a great number of choices when deciding what kind of containers into which you can put your syrup. The bottom line for most people will come down to cost, aesthetics and practicality. In order of preference, I prefer plastic, metal and then glass. I will discuss the reasons for selecting one bottling material over another next.

GLASS

In terms of shapes and sizes, glass containers offer the greatest number of shapes to consider. You could put your syrup in something as humble as a 1 pint canning jar, or you could spring for fancy flasks or those cute little bottles shaped like maple leaves. If your plan is to give some of your syrup as a gift, it's hard to argue with the maple leaf bottle, but if economy is your goal, keep in mind those little bottles can be pricey. As an example, the 500 ml (16.9 ounce) size is around $4, while a 12-ounce glass flask will cost about $1.50 each. Labels, stickers and lids will further add to your cash outlay. In the past, I've used 12-ounce flasks for my state fair entries, but for practical purposes, I think glass containers have several drawbacks.

ABOUT GLASS CONTAINERS:

- Glass bottles cost more than plastic jugs or metal cans.

- If you drop a hot glass bottle on the floor it will most likely shatter.

- If your filtering efforts are not quite as rigorous as they should be, once the syrup cools, the remaining nitre will settle to the bottom and it won't look very appealing in a clear, glass container.

- Bottles require packing in bubble wrap if you intend to ship them.

- If you have hard water, glass containers must be washed and sterilized in distilled water to prevent an accumulation of hard water scale — which is another expense you'll need to factor into your budget.

- Metal lids and rings, or metal screw on caps are more expensive than plastic ones.

- Glass requires extra storage considerations as sunlight and UV rays will cause the color and taste of syrup to deteriorate — much the same way as what happens to fine wines or beer.

- Continued sterilization and reuse of glass containers over time will result in glass fatigue, meaning a bigger chance that one might shatter when filled with hot syrup.

Sadly, this last point is from personal experience. While filling several pint sized canning jars, an "invisible" crack formed around the bottom of one of them. The jar filled properly and I was able to attach the lid and ring, but when I lifted the container to invert it, the entire bottom gave way and out poured 16 ounces of hot syrup all over everything. Not only did I lose a pint of hard-earned syrup, but also the kitchen was a mess! This was not what I needed to deal with at the end of a 16-hour workday that had commenced at 4 a.m.

PLASTIC

For a host of reasons, I prefer putting my syrup up in plastic jugs.

THE VIRTUES OF PLASTIC CONTAINERS:

- Hard water stains do not show on plastic bottles.

- Plastic is mostly unbreakable if dropped and very durable for shipping.

- If any nitre does settle out, if it wasn't filtered well enough, nobody will see it (including you).

- Plastic jugs can arrive pre-labeled another cost and task which can be avoided.

- Plastic screw-on jug lids cost less than glass or metal lids.

- Plastic containers are available in many more size options — ranging from four ounces up to five gallon sizes.

- Plastic is impervious to sunlight and prevents UV damage.

- Considering basic costs, the price of a pint size plastic jug is 75 percent less than a 500 ml maple leaf glass bottle.

Examples of syrup bottling container choices: 12-ounce glass flask, metal canister, 1 pint plastic jug and glass canning jar with their corresponding lids.

METAL CANS

While not as popular as they once were, syrup can be put into metal tins. Some can be found that are shaped like miniature sugar houses and have painted labels, others in plainer can styles can be purchased in round or rectangular shapes. All metal can types are sold with lids. Typically, metal cans range from 4 ounce to 500 ml (16.9 ounce) sizes.

CHOOSING METAL CONTAINERS:

- When compared to the 500 ml maple leaf glass bottle, the 500 ml metal can costs approximately fifty percent less.

- Metal is easy to sterilize.

- Like plastic, metal provides good sunlight and UV protection.

- There are no worries about hard water stains showing when using metal containers.

- Any settled out nitre remains very hidden from view.

- Metal cans may dent but they are usually unbreakable if dropped.

- Easy to pack and ship, metal cans are very attractive for gift giving.

- There are no extra expenses for the lids when using metal cans.

- Metal containers can be reused, but not indefinitely as the metal will begin to rust over time.

STERILIZING CONTAINERS

Whichever type of container you use, before bottling they must all be sterilized. I immerse my containers in a boiling water bath for 20 minutes. If I'm using glass canning jars, I sterilize the metal lids in boiling water as well. It's not advisable to do this with flask caps or plastic jug caps though, as the boiling water will loosen the inner safety seal.

When removing the items from the boiling water bath, it helps if you have a set of canning jar tongs, a magnetic lid lifter and possibly a wide-mouth funnel. These items can usually be found anywhere that canning supplies are sold. And they're equally handy if you'll be making jam too. Be sure to pour out the water from inside the containers as well. If it's not quite time to fill the containers with maple syrup yet, cover them with a clean cloth towel.

f you are going to be filling jugs or flask bottles, the job of pouring the sap is easier if it is first transferred into a saucepan that has a pouring spout. It also helps to have someone with a strong and steady hand doing the pouring.

When bottling the hot syrup, fill each container up to about ⅛ inch from the top. Wipe up any syrup from the container rim with a clean, damp cloth and immediately screw on the lid. Then invert the container for about five minutes. This will allow the inner safety seal in the lid to attach itself to the top of the container. After five minutes, flip the containers back upright. If you are using glass canning jars, listen for the "tink" sound as the metal lid snaps down as a result of a slight vacuum that has formed inside the jar as it cools. To protect your syrup, store the containers in a cool, dark place — especially if using clear glass jars.

Now it's time to clean up the kitchen and call it a productive day of getting ready to sugar off.

Jelly making jar tongs, magnetic lid lifter and wide-mouth funnel all work well for syrup bottling too.

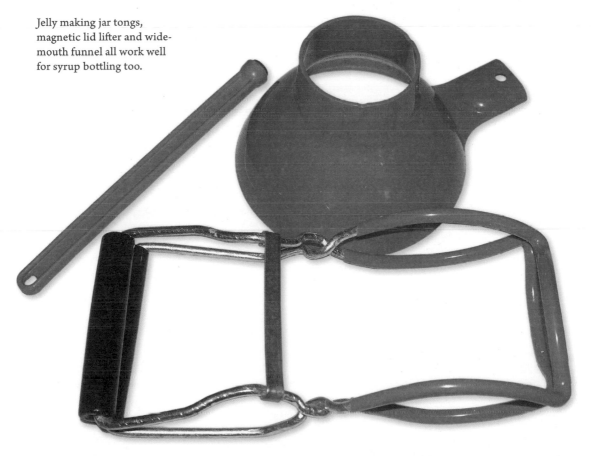

CHAPTER 13

THE END OF SUGAR SEASON TASKS

A S FEBRUARY MELTS into March and then gently morphs into hints of Spring in April, subtle chemical changes have begun to occur inside maple trees. After eight to ten weeks of the "sap running" up the trees from the roots to the branch tips, the food supply stored in the roots has been depleted, the branch tips have been given a heavy infusion of liquids and food, and the leaf buds have begun to swell. Daytime and nighttime temperatures have become much warmer and the maple sugar season is fast drawing to a close. The little bit of sap still running has probably developed a faint greenish cast.

Ah, the glaring pitfalls of buckets... Because buckets are not translucent, each must be inspected visually, which will become incredibly time consuming. Notice too that this young girl has nothing to transfer the contents of a filled bucket into. Worse yet, given her height, it's doubtful she could lift a filled bucket (45 pounds) off the spile to begin with.

BUD SAP

Then one day when you check the jugs or pails, all you will find is a bright yellow sap — called the "bud sap." When the bud sap arrives, the tree has begun sending up budding hormone, a chemical message that tells the leaves that it is time to burst free of their outer bud scales and unfurl. This signifies that the sugaring season is over.

If your tree tap holes haven't stopped running on their own, they soon will. Since bud sap is totally unsuitable for boiling, why wait any longer, go ahead and pull (remove) the taps. Once the hole is exposed to the air, it will stop dripping in a few hours and begin healing naturally. I usually don't wait for the bud sap to arrive. If I've already produced a good season's worth of syrup, I pull my taps during the last boil. That way I won't end up with sap I don't need. If I have a few gallons of sap that time constraints did not allow to be boiled off, I give it to a commercial producer that I know. This is better than having it spoil or go to waste. And over time, this practice has built up some good relationships that have given me a bit of leverage if I need a favor. Believe me, it's a good idea to cultivate the friendship of a nearby commercial producer. As a group, they have a fantastic pool of knowledge and if you're just starting out, their advice can help you avoid many setbacks.

END OF SEASON CLEANUP

Unlike the beginning of sugaring season when events like tapping and sap storage take place in stages, at the end of the season everything comes to a close at once. After the last boil has been completed, every piece of equipment must be thoroughly cleaned before storing. And despite the modest size of my little 24-tap operation, I'm always amazed at the amount of stuff I have to wash, scrub and dry. As I said earlier, sugaring is hard work, but at least when cleanup is finally over, it's done for another year. So here is some practical advice I have found that works best for cleaning your gear.

Unlike the beginning of sugaring season when events like tapping and sap storage take place in stages, at the end of the season everything comes to a close at once.

SPILES

Scrub your metal spiles with baking soda, using an old toothbrush or spout brush. Rinse them in hot water and let each dry thoroughly. To prevent rust from forming, after drying, coat each with vegetable oil and store in a dry place.

PLASTIC TAPS AND CONNECTORS

With a toothpick or bristled spout brush, gently scrub out the spouts and insides of your plastic connectors and taps. This will loosen any accumulated residue. Next, place them in the silverware basket of your dishwasher and wash them on the "hot" cycle with no soap. Alternatively, swish them around a washtub filled with very hot water and then let them soak. Set them aside to dry thoroughly both inside and out. When dry, place them in a zippered storage bag and tuck them away till next spring.

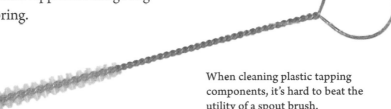

When cleaning plastic tapping components, it's hard to beat the utility of a spout brush.

PLASTIC ONE-GALLON MILK JUGS

Wash each jug in hot, soapy water, then rinse thoroughly. Invert them and allow to air dry completely. If any are showing stubborn mildew stains, send them on a well-deserved trip to the recycling center. You've got a whole year ahead to find replacement jugs. Be sure to wash and air dry the lids too. Admittedly, plastic jugs take up quite a bit of storage space. To minimize the vertical storage space they take up, you can tie a long piece of cord to the handle of one jug and thread the line through the handles of the others. The jugs can be stored in a "daisy chain" and hung in the garage or attic.

PLASTIC FIVE-GALLON WATER JUGS

Cleaning 5-gallon plastic jugs presents a bit more of a challenge because of their larger size. Fill the jug partially full with hot water, screw on the cap, shake vigorously, and then rinse. If interior stains or mildew are present, a long-handled bottle brush works wonders at reaching tough to access areas inside the jugs. After cleaning, invert each jug allowing them to air dry thoroughly.

SAP BUCKETS

Wash sap buckets thoroughly with warm, soapy water and dishwashing detergent, rinse them and towel dry to remove all traces of moisture. Then stack them upside down pyramid-style to thoroughly dry. For stubborn sticky spots, a bit of souring might be needed. If you have galvanized

A bottle brush may be necessary to clean a plastic five-gallon jug.

pails, use a plastic scouring pad or else you risk scarring the galvanized coating — which will lead to rusting. If you have stainless steel buckets, a copper scouring pad and some non-abrasive cleaner will shine them up nicely. Before deploying your sap buckets the next spring, check for any signs of mildew and clean them again if necessary.

> If properly cared for at seasons end, you can expect to get about 3 to 4 seasons out of your fabric filtering cone.

FABRIC FILTERS

Soak your fabric filtering cones in warm water to clean them. If the water becomes cloudy with the removed nitre, change it and continue soaking. When the fabric material is clean, squeeze (don't wring) the excess water out and hang them up to air dry before storing them away. If properly cared for at seasons end, you can expect to get about 3 to 4 seasons out of you fabric filtering cone.

PRE-HEATER

If you have a commercially manufactured reservoir pan, scrub the unit with either baking soda or a non-abrasive cleanser. Be sure to clean the feed line as well. To do this, open the valve, run hot water through it and scour the outside until it shines. Dry both the feed line and pre-heater well. For storage, wrap the feed line in a clean towel, set it inside the reservoir and place the reservoir in a clean plastic bag. If your pre-heater is a makeshift recycled ground coffee plastic container, wash it with plenty of hot water and dry it thoroughly. If you kept the plastic lid for the coffee container, you can use this for storing your taps and connectors until next spring.

SKIMMER

Using an old toothbrush and baking soda scrub any cooked-on nitre from the metal surfaces. Rinse the skimmer in hot water and dry well. You may wish to apply a light coating of olive oil to the wooden handle to prevent it from drying out and cracking. After drying and oiling the skimmer, wrap it in a clean towel and tuck it away with your other sugaring equipment.

EVAPORATOR

There are two cleaning chores to do with the evaporator pan. You'll need to remove the accumulated soot from the underside of the pan and the sticky sugar residue from the inside. To clean outside of my stainless steel evaporator, I take the pan to a coin operated car wash and spray the bottom with the high-pressure water. This blasts away most of the heavy soot — though sadly, some staining always remains. These soot stains, and the inside cooked-on surfaces require scouring with a copper scouring pad and non-abrasive cleanser. Scouring out the evaporator is generally thought of as the worst part of the end of season cleanup because you've got tough nitre deposits glued on with hard, caramelized sugar. It's best to do your evaporator scrubbing outside, even if you have to wait a bit for some warmer weather because the unit is big and bulky and awkward to scrub at the kitchen sink. After the evaporator is clean, towel dry most of the moisture off and then let it sit to air dry totally before encasing it in a large plastic bag. If your evaporator pan is a galvanized washtub, you've still got to scour it clean, but avoid using anything except a plastic scouring pad or you'll likely scratch the zinc coating.

AUGER

Although you may have cleaned your auger once when the tapping was completed, considering its replacement cost — check your auger once more. Give it another liberal coating of vegetable oil, wrap it up and store it away. Once your evaporator is clean and dried, you might use it as storage for small loose items such as your auger, taps and the like.

PLASTIC TUBING

While scouring and scrubbing the evaporator is a messy task at best, cleaning the lengths of plastic tubing is more nettlesome than anything else. If you've employed the "half n' half" method of sap collection that I use, it's not that hard to accomplish. Start by straightening a wire coat hanger and forming a tiny loop at one end. Tear a thin strip of terrycloth and attach a string to each end. Wet the cloth with the hottest water you can draw from the faucet. Tie one string on the terrycloth to the coat hanger loop, leaving the other string loose from the other end of the terrycloth. Pass the coat hanger through the tube, pulling the terrycloth through to the other end. Then pull the terrycloth back using the free string. A few trips back and forth through each tube will usually clean them thoroughly. However, it you encounter a length of plastic tubing clouded from UV exposure or badly fouled with mildew, it's time to bid farewell to that section. Given the relatively low cost of a roll of tubing and the short lengths used in my system, it's not worth my time to put in lots of extra effort to clean really tough jobs. Unfortunately, like frosty night air, mildew is free too.

STORAGE TANK

If you opted for a 65-gallon storage tank, you've got your work cut out for you. Fill it with water (preferably warm water), insert your arm into the fill port and scrub every surface you can reach with a long-handled brush. Drain the tank, wipe out the inside to remove as much moisture as possible, invert it in a warm, sunny location and wait for the remaining contents to drip out or evaporate. Once it's completely dry inside, and assuming you can find a large enough plastic bag, cover it until next season. The same advice applies if you used a plastic garbage can and plastic hose bib for sap storage. And whatever you do, don't use the sugaring garbage can for any other purpose besides storing sap (and for that matter any of your other sugaring equipment too).

A 65-gallon storage tank.

RECORDING DETAILS

Though not an absolute requirement for the successful backyard producer, I would strongly suggest setting up a detailed log of your syrup-related expenses and your annual production figures. And at the end of the season this is the time to do it if you haven't done it already. As your experience and sugar making skill grows, a diligently maintained written record will enable you to track your progress over time. A basic spreadsheet might include the following:

- CALENDAR YEAR
- TAPPING DATE
- NUMBER OF TAPS DEPLOYED
- BOILING DATE(S)
- QUANTITY OF SYRUP PRODUCED
  (I list mine in pints)
- SYRUP GRADE
- TOTAL PRODUCTION FOR THE YEAR
- NOTES OR COMMENTS

CHAPTER 14

BUILD YOUR OWN SUSTAINABILITY NETWORK

· ·

LOOKING BACK 150 years, nearly every American lived on a family farm. The family was very self-sufficient and raised their own livestock, vegetables, grain and forage. They cut their own wood, tended their own orchards or fruit-bearing plants, sheared their own sheep, and some even made their own maple syrup. Every individual and family, other than the 10 percent that lived in cities, strived to achieve a high level of self-sufficiency. But not everyone could master all the skills needed to be totally self-sufficient. The orchard man might have been a poor hand at raising livestock, but he still needed meat. The beekeeper also kept a few chickens, but had too many eggs for one family. the woodcutter had no talent for farming, but made maple syrup every spring, and his raspberries were the best anyone had eever tasted. But a person can't very well ilve on a diet consisting entirely of syrup and berries. Even in 1861, people specialized in what each knew best. But specialization is both a blessing and a curse, because you've got a "longage" of what *you* can produce and a glaring shortage of everything else. Now, just as it was in those times, everyone is good at something, but almost no one is proficient at everything.

BARTERING

So how did everyone survive back then? Easy. They bartered what they had for what they needed. Remember, most rural landowners were as cash-strapped back then as many are today. Our ancestors developed and used a simple formula: no money changed hands and everyone got a fair shake. That's how true communities are formed — mutual need and mutual benefit. Think of their system of exchange as socialism without the taxes, communism without the torture, or capitalism without the money. A community is not a legally defined gio-political entity; in its purest form it's a network of people sharing what they have for the things they desire.

> This community, in its purest form, is a network of people sharing what they have and trading for the things they don't have and thusly desire.

How times have changed, or have they? Lately, the press is filled with stories extolling the virtues of sustainability, while urging support of local farmers and at the same time imploring consumers to regain control of what they eat. And up to a point, there's much to be admired about those currently trendy points of view. But, I'm not a big fan of media hype or "environmentally conscious" buzzwords, because while buzzwords come and go, basic human needs and the desire to fulfill them are as old as the human race itself. So what's this got to do with making maple syrup? Simple.

As a backyard syrup maker, your annual production *might* total six gallons. And unless you eat French toast for breakfast every morning, it's doubtful you'll use all that syrup before sugar time comes around again. But maple syrup

has tremendous value. As an example, one website I found online (and absolutely refuse to name) sells 8-ounce bottles for $14.95, and that doesn't even include the shipping charges!

Have you got enough of your own syrup to sell? That's doubtful, and besides, unless it's inspected by the agriculture department or its equivalent in your state, it's probably not legal for you to sell it anyway. But assuming it was inspected, and assuming you put it all up in 8-ounce bottles, even at $15 at a whack, you're still only looking at a revenue total of about $900. Worse yet, if you sell it all you won't have any syrup left for yourself! So rather than ending up with money and no syrup, why not try to build a community food network like the one I belong to? Including myself, my community network of sustainability has seven members. And basically, here's how it works.

COMMUNITY SUSTAINABILITY NETWORK

I swap syrup for honey with my neighbor up the road. He owns less than an acre of land, heats with a wood-burning stove, but has no woodlot. However, he keeps bees and I have a large black locust woodlot, the flower nectar of which makes incredible tasting honey. Another neighbor, about equidistand the other direction, plants a quarter-acre garden and boards horses. He has no maple trees but plenty of manure. A third guy, a bit farther down the road, raises strawberries. Around the first corner from my house lives a fellow whose expertise at growing apples is very well known. Another neighbor about a mile away raises chickens. I make maple syrup, own a 45-acre woodlot, and maintain a luxuriant black-berry patch.

Get the picture? The seven of us didn't arrive

simultaneously on the country road we share and we devoted considerable time getting to know each other. But once that happened we discovered to our mutual advantage that we could engage in a network of old-fashioned, cash-free country commerce to benefit us all. The math isn't important. It's the sense of community and trust that's important. We each exchange goods with one another, have become good neighbors, and in some cases close friends.

Trust is the lynchpin. Our simple barter-based system couldn't exist without it. My beekeeper friend has no honey in March, but he receives maple syrup from me, as do the apple grower, strawberry patch owner, and the vegetable gardener. After I deliver my maple syrup, I won't receive any return of honey, fruit or vegetables for several months to come. So I have to trust that the bonds I've built will hold tight. The chicken guy won't be canning any of my blackberries until late July, but despite that, I can still rely on receiving my regular allotment of eggs, because he trusts me. Remove mutual trust from our little economic model, and the thing collapses like a house of cards.

Can you and your neighbors emulate our enterprise? I don't know. What I do know is that you'd be a fool if you didn't try.

Lastly, from a sustainability standpoint, it's nearly impossible to think of anything *more* sustainable than making your own maple syrup. Unlike a garden that must be replanted annually or chickens that must be replaced as the older hens end up on the chopping block, once a sugar maple tree reaches the minimum tapping diameter of 16 inches, it may be tapped annually for the next 100 years or more.

From a sustainability standpoint, it's nearly impossible to think of anything more sustainable than making your own maple syrup.

CHAPTER 15

BASIC EQUIPMENT COSTS

W HETHER YOUR PASSION is playing golf, boating, hunting or the like, to properly engage in any of these pursuits, you've got to spend money on equipment and supplies. You could easily spend thousands on golf clubs and balls to smack into water hazards, and a decent hunting rifle plus ammunition could cost at least this much too. You can't break par or put meat on the table without paying for some tools to do each of these activities. Along that same vein, I've assembled a basic sugaring equipment and supplies list that I have added some current pricing information. Bear in mind, though, that this

The author and sugaring partner Pauly, right, with a soot-covered washtub.

is a basic list to get you started. Later if you want to own a fancy bottling tank or other optional accessories, you're on your own.

Lastly, these prices are for new equipment. You may be able to acquire some used items through the classified ads or by searching the Internet. And unless otherwise noted, these prices are for a single item. If you opt for a 24-tap system, like mine, you'll have to do the math for your budget, but you may be entitled to discounts if you buy in quantity.

Also note, as I researched prices, I discovered wide disparities between various retailers, so check several and do plenty of comparison shopping. This is another reason why planning far in advance is advisable. There's no reason to spend more money than necessary.

BASIC EQUIPMENT COSTS

TAPS AND TUBING:

- 7/16-inch steel spiles, $2.75
- 5/16-inch aluminum taps (used with sap bags), $2.40
- 5/16-inch plastic bucket taps, $2.05
- 7/16-inch plastic tubing taps, 48¢
- 5/16-inch plastic tubing taps, 39¢
- "T" connector, 24¢
- Straight tubing connector, 32¢
- Plastic tubing (100-foot roll), $15.00

AUGERS AND DRILLS:

- 7/16-inch auger $13.50
- 5/16-inch auger, $13.50
- 7/16-inch twist drill bit, $26.00
- 5/16-inch twist drill bit, $17.50

SAP COLLECTION EQUIPMENT:

- 9-quart galvanized sap bucket, $19.50
- 9-quart galvanized sap bucket (used), $2.00 & up
- 16-quart galvanized sap bucket, $19.50
- 16-quart stainless-steel sap bucket, $85.00
- Metal bucket lids, $4.00
- Metal bucket lids (used), $2.00
- 3-gallon plastic sap buckets, $8.50
- Plastic bucket lids, $3.60
- 1-gallon milk jugs, free
- 5-gallon frying oil jugs, free
- 4-gallon drinking water bottles, free

SAP STORAGE EQUIPMENT:

- 65-gallon storage tank with draw-off valve, $200.00
- 35-gallon plastic garbage can, $19.00
- Plastic faucet (hose bib), $4.00
- 1-gallon milk jugs, free
- 5-gallon frying oil jugs, free
- 4-gallon drinking water bottles, free

EVAPORATOR PANS:

- 12-gallon galvanized washtub, $23.00

BOTTLING/CANNING CONTAINERS:

- 1-pint plastic syrup jug, $1.01
- 12-ounce flask style bottle, $1.37
- 500-ml (16.9 ounces) glass maple leaf bottle, $4.05
- 500-ml (16.9 ounces) metal syrup can, $2.25
- One dozen 16-ounce canning jars, rings & lids, $9.49

ACCESSORIES:

- Dacron filtering cones (1 dozen per package), $17.50
- 5-quart wool felt filtering cone, $23.50
- 2-gallon synthetic filtering cone, $13.50
- Candy thermometer, $20.50
- 3-inch dial thermometer, $52.00
- Digital thermometer, $89.00
- Test cup, $27.00
- Hydrometer, $11.50
- Foam skimmer, $54.00
- Hardwood skimmer handle, $11.00
- ½-inch brass ball valve draw-off faucet, $25.00
- Syrup grading kit, $28.50
- Heavy-duty work gloves, $15.00
- Spout brush, $3.50
- Leader "Half Pint" evaporator kit, $1,099.00

LEADER EVAPORATOR KIT:

This evaporator kit includes the following components:

- Three-section evaporator pan & draw-off valve

- Reservoir tank & feed line/valve

- Instruction/assembly manual

Note: This evaporator unit is shipped via UPS ground and requires about two hours to assemble. The kit does not include fire brick, fire brick cement, or stove pipe. This price also does not include shipping charges or sales tax.

EVAPORATOR KIT NECESSITIES:

- Full-size fire brick: 4½" x 9" x 2½", $2.50

- Half-size fire brick: 4½" x 9" x 1¼", $2.30

- Refractory cement (1-gallon container), $23.00

- Fire tool or poker, $12.00

Note: fire brick, cement, pokers and related items can usually be purchased from any retailer selling wood stoves or fireplace inserts.

After 20 years of sugaring, there are many seasons when I don't buy any supplies at all.

Unless you intend to install your "Half Pint" evaporator in a permanent building like a sugar house or utility shed, I'd recommend mounting the unit on a homemade dolly. I built mine using 2 x 6 lumber, sixteen ⅜-inch carriage bolts, and four swiveling casters. Then, with the arch still empty, I lag screwed it onto the dolly. After it was secured, I added my fire brick, insulating sand and a steel grate. It's important to perform these steps in that order, because after you add fire brick to the arch, it will doubtless be too heavy to maneuver atop the dolly. When it's time to boil, I simply roll the unit outside, level it, lay a good fire, and begin boiling.

Another thing to keep in mind is that while your initial cash outlay for sugaring supplies and equipment might seem a trifle steep, items like plastic taps, connectors, jugs and the like can be reused indefinitely. Amortized over time, your cash outlay will actually diminish. After 20 years of sugaring, there are many seasons when I don't buy any supplies at all.

Just like I was back in the early days, you've no doubt already been bitten by the sugaring bug or you wouldn't be reading this book. Congratulations on taking the initial steps needed to become a sugar maker. I wish you the very best of good fortune and here's hoping you produce the best tasting maple syrup ever. Now get to work and make the rest of us sugar makers proud.

Fully stoked and boiling away, my small backyard evaporator unit is working hard on another batch of golden delicious maple syrup. Note my homemade dolly for easy maneuvering.

RESOURCES

ADDITIONAL SUGARING RESOURCES

COUNTRYSIDE HARDWARE
1712 Albany Street
DeRuyter, New York 13052
Phone: 315-852-3326
www.countrysidehardware.com

LEADER EVAPORATOR CO., INC.
49 Jonergin Drive
Swanton, Vermont 05488
Phone: 802-868-5444
www.leaderevaporator.com

LEHMAN'S
One Lehman Circle
P.O. Box 270
Kidron, Ohio 44636
Phone: 877-438-5346
www.lehmans.com

ONTARIO ORCHARDS
7735 Route 104
Southwest Oswego, New York 13126
Phone: 315-343-6328
www.ontarioorchards.com

WRIGHTWAY HARDWARE
WRIGHT'S CORNERS

9236 Oswego Road (New York Route 48)
Baldwinsville, New York 13027
Phone: 315-695-2394
Email: *www.wrightwayhardware@yahoo.com*

TRACTOR SUPPLY CO.

Several hundred locations nationwide.
Phone: 877-718-6750
www.tractorsupply.com

NOTE: Lehman's, Countryside Hardware and Leader
Evaporator Co. will ship product directly to your door.
Because Lehman's sells primarily to Amish farmers who
eschew electricity and modern products, its selection of
sugaring supplies/equipment is understandably limited.
In addition to its website, Lehman's also publishes a 170-
page full-color catalog which they will mail to you upon
request.

LEADER EVAPORATOR CO. has an extensive authorized
dealer network throughout the Northeast and upper
Midwest. The Leader website can assist you in locating
the dealer closest to you. Leader also maintains a retail
store in Rutland, Vermont. As items become available,
Leader's website also contains listings for both used and
factory second-grade equipment. Periodically the site also
advertises clearance items.

BOTH LEHMAN'S & COUNTRYSIDE are open to the
public for retail sales as well. Though I reside about 75
miles from Countryside Hardware, I make the drive every

three to four years to stock up on syrup jugs, lids and other supplies. On other occasions, I shop locally at the Wrightway or Ontario Orchards. However, Countryside is somewhat unique in that it not only sells sugaring supplies and equipment, the owners are also syrup producers themselves. And while I've been sugaring for more than 20 years, I still find it helpful to have access to their considerable expertise. To me, the best feature about the place is that they sell a range of quantities, both case lots to large commercial operations, and amateurs like me can buy a single item.

IF THE DISTANCE is not prohibitively long, I recommend an in-person visit to any of the places I've listed, especially if you're just starting out. It's always nice to be able to look at sugaring supplies where you can pick them up and examine them firsthand; something you just can't do at a website.

TRACTOR SUPPLY does not sell sugaring equipment *per se*, but it does carry such items as storage tanks, augers and plastic tubing.

LASTLY, the retailer names and web addresses I've listed should not be construed as an all-inclusive group, or any type of veiled commercial endorsement. In a word, I don't shill, period. The names merely represent the folks I've done business with over the years and keep coming back to time and again.

Your local hardware may carry sugaring supplies and equipment as well. With the increased emphasis placed on shopping locally, your hometown merchant is an excellent place to begin seeking out sugaring supplies and equipment.

ADDITIONAL READING

"SUGAR TIME PRIMER"
This broad overview of the entire sugaring process appeared in the March/April 2011 issue of *BackHome* magazine. A back issue is available for purchase at the magazine's website, *www.backhomemagazine.com*.

BACKHOME MAGAZINE
P.O. Box 70
Hendersonville, North Carolina 28793
Phone: 800-992-2546 or 828-696-3838
Fax: 828-696-0700
www.backhomemagazine.com

NATIONAL AUDUBON SOCIETY FIELD GUIDE TO NORTH AMERICAN TREES
(Eastern Region); Alfred A. Knopf, Inc;
Elbert L. Little; 1980

ADDITIONAL MAPLE TREE FACTS & PHOTOS

USDA Plant Guide; Sugar Maple
www.plants.usda.gov/plantguide/pdf/pg_acsa3.pdf

USDA Plant Guide; Red Maple:
www.plants.usda.gov/plantguide/pdf/pg_acru.pdf

Maple Field Guide; Black Maple:
www.mapleinfo.org/htm/blackm.cfm

MAPLE FESTIVALS & SUGAR SHACK OPEN HOUSES

During March and April each year, numerous states hold maple festivals. Additionally, many maple producers' associations hold open house weekends when commercial syrup operations open their doors to the general public. As a backyard amateur or someone aspiring to become one, these events offer a golden opportunity to ask a ton of questions to experienced professional sugar makers. I've listed the names and websites of several below. For times and locations of local or regional events, check your community newspaper. I would encourage you to attend all that you can. Knowledge is power.

THE NATIONAL MAPLE SYRUP FESTIVAL
Medora, Indiana
www.nationalmaplesyrupfestival.com

CONNECTICUT MAPLE SYRUP FESTIVALS
www.connecticutmaplesyrupfestival.com

MAINE MAPLE SYRUP FESTIVALS
www.mainemaplesyrupfestival.com

MASSACHUSETTS MAPLE SYRUP FESTIVALS
www.massachusettsmaplesyrupfestival.com

MICHIGAN MAPLE SYRUP FESTIVALS
www.michiganmaplesyrupfestival.com

MINNESOTA MAPLE SYRUP FESTIVALS
www.minnesotamaplesyrupfestival.com

FESTIVALS

NEW HAMPSHIRE MAPLE FESTIVALS

www.newhampshiremaplesyrupfestival.com

NEW YORK STATE MAPLE PRODUCERS ASSOCIATION

www.nysmaple.com

MAPLE WEEKEND (NEW YORK STATE)

www.mapleweekend.com

OHIO MAPLE SYRUP FESTIVALS

www.ohiomaplesyrupfestival.com

PENNSYLVANIA MAPLE FESTIVAL

Meyersdale, Pennsylvania
www.pamaplefestival.com

PICKENS WEST VIRGINIA MAPLE SYRUP FESTIVAL

www.pickenswv.squarespace.com/maple-syrup-festival

VERMONT MAPLE FESTIVAL

www.vtmaplefestival.org

WISCONSIN MAPLE SYRUP FESTIVALS & PRODUCERS

www.wisconsinmaplesyrupfestival.com

JACK WAX

No book about maple syrup would be complete without the "recipe" for Jack Wax. So here it is. Spread a layer of finely crushed/shaved ice on a frozen cookie sheet. Drizzle some warm syrup across the ice. The liquid will immediately congeal into beautiful amber strands or globs of super sweet, super sticky Jack Wax. Delicious and messy, but most delicious!

INDEX

INTERIOR PHOTOGRAPH CREDITS

NOTES

ABOUT ACRES U.S.A.

*A*cres U.S.A. is the national magazine of organic/ sustainable agriculture. In this exploding field, *Acres U.S.A* is alone as a publication with a real track record — 40+ years of continuous publication.

More than a "theories" magazine, *Acres U.S.A.* brings you practical, hands-on information that you can immediately put to work on your farm.

You'll meet successful, chemical-free operations and visit their farms through on-the-scene case reports.

Every month a leading figure in eco-agriculture tells it like it is in the *Acres U.S.A.* Interview. They hand off advice, expose you to new ideas, or explain the top issues facing agriculture today.

Finally, *Acres U.S.A.* strives to be a one-stop information source for the issues of ecological farming and living, offering a free catalog of over 400 books on subjects ranging from crops and soils to animal and human health. You'll never find a more complete listing of hard-to-find books on all the subjects you're most interested in. Request a copy today!